Looking Through
the Cross

LOOKING THROUGH THE CROSS

THE ARCHBISHOP OF CANTERBURY'S LENT BOOK 2014

GRAHAM TOMLIN

BLOOMSBURY

LONDON • NEW DELHI • NEW YORK • SYDNEY

First published in Great Britain 2013

Copyright © Graham Tomlin, 2013

The moral right of the author has been asserted

A Continuum book

Bloomsbury Publishing Plc
50 Bedford Square
London WC1B 3DP

www.bloomsbury.com

Bloomsbury Publishing, London, New Delhi, New York and Sydney

A CIP record for this book is available from the British Library.

ISBN 978-1-4081-8847-7

10 9 8 7 6 5 4 3 2 1

Typeset by Fakenham Prepress Solutions, Fakenham, Norfolk
NR21 8NN

Printed and Bound in Great Britain by CPI Group (UK) Ltd,
Croydon, CR0 4YY

CONTENTS

FOREWORD BY THE ARCHBISHOP OF CANTERBURY

The crucifixion of Jesus Christ is the great mystery of the Christian Faith. It is a mystery because everything about it points in the wrong direction. For God to be fully human, and then to die an ignominious death reserved for a criminal, seems so extraordinary and pointless as to be inexplicable. Indeed in the early centuries of Christianity many of the accusations against the church started with the assumption that you could not seriously believe in a God who undertook such a terrible and dishonourable death.

The truth of the crucifixion is shown as much as anything by the fact that the early church, despite these attacks, stuck to the story come what may. In John's Gospel the cross and the story of the crucifixion are seen as the triumphant point in the life of Jesus. In none of the Gospels is it considered at any point to be defeat.

For people then and now the call to become a disciple of Jesus Christ was not found in a set of principles and ethics but in encountering Him so that he becomes known as both God and also as Friend, extremes held together most beautifully in the Gospel of St John. The true depth of friendship is seen in its transforming impact on our lives and behaviour. The radical nature of the love of Christ has to be lived in relationship with Him, not merely learned in observation of Him, let alone in knowledge of His words. Because He is God, and also Friend, we are touched at the depth of our beings as we live with Him through every event of His birth, life, trial, death, resurrection and ascension.

The cross is the moment of deepest encounter and most radical change. God is crucified – my Friend died – in some way, for me. Merely writing or reading these words together in one sentence is overwhelming. A person caught by the implications of the cross will be a person who has found the fullness of the life which is the gift of God.

Two thousand years later, the cross has lost much of its capacity to shock and to challenge. For those early Christians it was a badge of shame. Today it is more commonly seen as a symbol of beauty to hang around your neck. As a friend of mine used to say, you might as well hang a tiny golden gallows or an electric chair around your neck.

Are we now living with a symbol emptied of power by time and fashion? Christianity with a powerless cross is Christianity without a throne for Christ or an aspiration for Christians. A cross that has no weight is not worth carrying. To look though the cross is to seek its weight.

Graham Tomlin explores the implications of the cross in this remarkable book. He is a first-class scholar, and does not ignore the challenges and problems that a crucified God raises in the 21st century. But from my own knowledge of him as a friend and adviser, I am aware that Graham shapes his own life and work around the cross. His whole person is, one might say, cross-shaped.

That combination of personal spirituality and considerable scholarship, together with the experience of running a church in the centre of London and leading a training college for those preparing for ordination, have all enabled him to reflect with realism, with relevance and with clarity on what the cross means.

In one way or another, Graham calls for us to see the cross as a starting point: not only for a view of ourselves but of the whole world. It transforms our living *and* our seeing. The invitation to write the book was given by my predecessor, Archbishop Rowan Williams, and I could not be more pleased that it should be published during my first year as his successor.

I encourage you to reflect on this book slowly – whether alone or in company – and to let its impact seep into you deeply. As Good Friday approaches – again and again – I long that it may jolt each and all of us to become people who see the world differently because we glimpse it afresh through Christ's cross. Because we choose to bear its weight.

The impact of the Cross has to be felt and reflected in each generation. Cross-shaped churches may be the architectural norm – but they are also the spiritual exception. Just as we each find the pattern of our lives too easily conforming to contemporary culture, so the pattern of the life of the church tends to do the same. We need to rethink what a cross-shaped church means in a very non-cross-shaped culture.

Finally, the cross stands for freedom at another's expense. In an age of self-fulfilment, to give up something as precious as one's future for another sounds insane. Graham contrasts cross and culture, cross and personal habits, and shows the attractiveness of cross. In it is all treasure. May Lent bring you that treasure.

+Justin Cantuar

INTRODUCTION

Looking is something we do all the time. From the moment we wake in the morning until we close our eyes before sleep at night, if we have the precious gift of sight, we spend all of our days looking at things. It is so natural a part of our lives that we barely consider it. It is the kind of action, like breathing or talking, that occurs unconsciously, without our noticing that we are doing it. At this very moment you are looking at this page, or perhaps a screen, if you happen to be reading this as an e-book. If you look up from where you are sitting or standing, as no doubt you will in a moment, to take a break from the concentrated focus of reading, you will be able to look at a whole range of things, people, buildings, landscapes.

Looking is different from seeing. Seeing is a more passive activity. We see a passing car, a dog on the pavement, a film at the cinema, a flock of birds in the sky. When we see things, we do not really consider them, or perhaps even think about them. We 'notice' them, observe them, perhaps register in our minds that we have 'seen' them, but little more. Looking is a more purposeful activity. When we look at our reflection in a mirror, at the cover of a book, or at a photograph in a magazine, we gaze a little more intently; we pause, focus and try to take in what we see.

And there are different ways of looking. We can look at things. When we do this, we focus our attention on the thing we are looking at. We might come across a striking statue in a museum or a town square. We might walk around it, considering it from all sides, seeing how it fits into its surroundings, examining its contours, colour and shape, wondering how it was made, pondering what it tells us about the sculptor or what it is trying to say about its subject. To look at something is to make it the focus of attention and to try to understand it on its own terms, or in its environment.

But that is different from looking *through* something. We look through a window, or a pair of spectacles. A little like seeing, with this kind of looking, we are barely aware that we are doing it. When you look through a window, you are rarely aware that you are doing so. You are gazing at the object you see out of the window. The point of the window is to enable us to see what is beyond it, but in such a fashion as to not get in the way, to provide a transparent view, and to give us a clear sight of what we are seeing. It is similar, but also a little different, when it comes to looking through spectacles. When I put on my glasses, as I do first thing in the morning, from that moment on, I am hardly aware that I am looking through them – they have just become part of the way I see. And yet I notice when I take them off. Everything then becomes blurred, uncertain, hazy. My glasses enable me to see, but not by giving a kind of neutral, transparent film, as a window does, but by actually changing the way I look at something. I do not 'see' my spectacles, I do not 'look at' them – I look through them, and in the very act of looking, they change the way I see the world.

Eastern Orthodox Christians make extensive use of icons in worship and prayer. To the untrained western eye, these look like images of Christ or the saints, to be looked at, studied or contemplated. Yet iconographers and ordinary Christians in the east insist that an icon is not something to be looked at, but looked through. There was an old test of whether an icon painter's work was valid as a true icon – can you pinch the nose of the figure in the icon between your thumb and forefinger? In other words, does anything stand out from the surface of the icon in such a way as to make it three-dimensional, rather than two-dimensional? An icon suitable for prayer or devotion very definitely needed just two-dimensions, not three.

Why? Because if an icon has three dimensions, it becomes an object. It becomes something to look at, to examine in itself. You can, as it were, walk around it and look at it. The icon itself becomes the focus of attention, its colour, beauty, sense of proportion and so on. On the other hand, if it has only two dimensions, it becomes something to look through, not at. A window has, as it were, only two dimensions – height and width – it does not really have depth, or at least, the depth is not important, as it is transparent. An icon of Christ is intended as a window into Christ, so that you look through the image to the real Christ beyond it.

At the same time (like the spectacles we considered just now) it shapes the way we look at Christ, by helping us see a distinct image of him. A three-dimensional icon can become no longer an icon but an idol. It becomes something that stops us looking at Christ and just our image of him, which is why the Old Testament, and many Christian traditions since then, warn against making images of God. Eastern Orthodox iconography can only avoid the charge of idolatry by maintaining this strict distinction between looking at and looking through.

This book is an act of two kinds of looking – looking at and looking through. First, it looks at the cross, trying to understand more about this strange idea, that (as Christian theology has always claimed) God the Father allowed his Son to die a gruesome and painful death. It tries to understand what that means and why it was in some sense necessary. The first two chapters therefore look at what the cross tells us about God and about ourselves.

The rest of the book is an exercise, not so much of looking at, but in looking through. It proceeds to view the cross, not only as an object to be studied or examined, but also as a lens through which we might look at the world. We will be trying to use the cross as a kind of lens through which to look at a whole series of aspects of contemporary life and experience. We will try to see how life looks when seen through the lens of the cross. It is in experiment in transparency, seeing the cross as an interpretive key for looking at the world.

Sometimes we have to look at a pair of spectacles or a pane of glass in a window to understand how it is made, why it works. To serve as a good pair of spectacles they need to work well, and so an understanding of how they work, how the frame fits the glass, how the glass is designed is vital. However, spectacles and windows are primarily for looking through, not at. In the same way, the cross repays close attention to help us see what it is, why it happened, and how it affects us. However, it also can serve to help us see the world differently. What might it mean to live in a world in which the Son of God gave himself up to death at the hands of human beings like you and me? What does that tell us, not just about God and ourselves, but about issues such as ambition, failure, weakness, suffering, society?

Looking through the cross is, in a way, an exercise that demands a certain kind of faith. Putting on a pair of spectacles can make the whole world look clearer and more distinct. Put on the wrong pair, and it makes it worse. Everything becomes more blurred and hazy. It can even give you a headache. How do we know whether 'looking through the cross' in this way will improve, not damage our vision? There are a number of voices that would argue that the cross, as a symbol of violence and punishment, is the last thing we should take as our key for looking at the world. We will be looking at these arguments from time to time as we go through this book. However for the time being, we have to just take a chance. How do you know whether a pair of spectacles will improve your vision? There is only one way: to try them on. This book is an exercise in doing just that.

As in any book, there are people to thank. First, my thanks are due to Bishop Rowan Williams, who invited me to write it. I was delighted to accept the invitation as a small act of thanks and gratitude for his wise and courageous leadership of the Anglican Church to which I belong, over recent years, and for the privilege of working with his wife Jane as a highly valued and wise colleague at St Paul's Theological Centre and St Mellitus College.

Justin Welby is now the Archbishop and this book comes with thanks to and prayers for him as he continues to provide bold and wise oversight of the church. Thanks are due too to all those at Continuum who helped the book emerge into the light, including Robin Baird-Smith, Nicola Rusk, and Caroline Chartres.

Many of the ideas in this book were first tried out in a series of meditations on successive Good Fridays in Holy Trinity Brompton, which has for the past eight years been a stimulating, lively and wonderful church to belong to. My thanks are also due to Simone Odendaal for her perceptive and efficient support, as well as my fellow faculty members at St Mellitus College with whom some of these ideas have been chewed over and discussed. They are more friends than colleagues, examples rather than employees, and I am deeply indebted to them.

I am also grateful for the comments of a few people who kindly gave time to read through the manuscript and suggest some changes before publication, including Simon Featherstone, Steve Gold, Ben Lovell, Keir Shreeves, Mia Smith, Matt Smith and Graham Stevenson.

As always my chief gratitude is for my family: for Janet, for Sam and Jenni, Sian and Josh, all seeking in some way or another to follow the way of the cross, and who bring me a great deal of life and love as they do so.

I

THE CROSS AND WISDOM

They took Jesus to the high priest, and
all the chief priests, the elders and the
teachers of the law came together ...
Very early in the morning, the chief
priests, with the elders, the teachers of
the law and the whole Sanhedrin, reached
a decision ... (Mk 14.53; 15.1)

For the message of the cross is foolishness
to those who are perishing, but to us
who are being saved it is the power of
God. For it is written: "I will destroy the
wisdom of the wise; the intelligence of
the intelligent I will frustrate." Where are
the wise? Where is the teacher of the law?
Where is the philosopher of this age? Has
not God made foolish the wisdom of the
world? For since in the wisdom of God
the world through its wisdom did not
know him, God was pleased through the
foolishness of what was preached to save
those who believe. Jews demand signs

and Greeks look for wisdom, but we
preach Christ crucified: a stumbling block
to Jews and foolishness to Gentiles, but
to those whom God has called, both Jews
and Greeks, Christ the power of God and
the wisdom of God. For the foolishness
of God is wiser than human wisdom, and
the weakness of God is stronger than
human strength. (1 Cor. 1.18–25)

A t one point in the long, involved and politi-
cally charged process through which Jesus
was executed, there is a classic confrontation. Jesus,
the accused, stands before the authorities who
hold his fate in their hands. The way Mark tells the
story heightens the sense of tension and conflict.
Jesus stands before the Jewish establishment of
his time: the religious authorities, the scholars,
the judges. The Sanhedrin was the Jewish ruling
council, which met in the Temple at Jerusalem,
the central place of Jewish life, to resolve disputes
over interpretation of the law in the land. They
were a kind of blend between a bench of bishops
and a supreme court, the ultimate religious and
legal authority. The 'teachers of the law' were
the scholars, the professors, those who knew the
ancient law inside out, and were charged with the

responsibility to interpret it in different situations. The chief priests were religious professionals, those who oversaw the worship of Israel in the Temple. Together, they represented a formidable set of opponents.

Jesus, the rabbi, the teacher of Israel, confronts the wise. This crisis brought together the best minds and the wisest counsel in Jerusalem at the time, to work out what to do with Jesus. And they talk past each other. They find him impossible to reason with, difficult to understand. Various witnesses, of dubious motive, are brought before the court to testify to Jesus' guilt, yet, faced with mounting evidence, he seems to act in a completely bizarre fashion. In Matthew's version of the story, Jesus just says nothing. Faced with a process that looks like it will lead inexorably to a painful and gruesome death, Jesus has nothing to say. When he does speak, what he says is enigmatic to say the least. When asked the direct question 'Are you the Messiah?' his answer is perplexing. Matthew's version has the enigmatic 'so you say'. Mark's version draws out a more direct claim, but still startling in its boldness: 'I am, and you will see the Son of Man sitting at the right hand of the Mighty One.' Either way, Jesus' answer is not designed to secure his release, as we might expect or even hope. In neither case does he give the expected denial, the properly self-deprecating response, shocked that anyone might suggest such a thing. If there was one central fact that the Sanhedrin and the teachers of the law knew, it was that God is One, and shares his glory with no other. To fit into that theological scheme, the obvious and anticipated answer at this point would be an expression of humility and deference. 'Are you the "Son of the Blessed One"? Of course not, I am just a prophet called to declare the word of the Lord.'

And yet that is precisely what Jesus does not say. He talks about sitting at the right hand of God, coming on the 'clouds of heaven', picking up the prophecy of Daniel 7 of the 'Son of Man', this figure destined for 'authority, glory and sovereign power'. The language is bold, startling and frankly, peculiar. This country rabbi, speaking before the experts in the law of Israel, claims that he will soon sit on a throne beside the God of Israel, surrounded by the trappings of glory and universal recognition. He is speaking a language they just do not understand. They might have expected a messiah, but not one that looked like this. Not surprisingly they conclude that he is talking at best nonsense, at worst blasphemy. When Jesus faces the wise, they can make no sense of him.

Paul, Jesus and the wise

A number of years later, Paul the disciple and interpreter of Jesus, reflecting perhaps on this very episode, also considers the nature of wisdom and the way in which Christian faith just does not fit with convention.

A few years earlier, around 50 AD, he had been involved in the founding of a new Christian community in the Greek city of Corinth. Now, a little later, as he writes to them, he has heard news that the Church has strayed from the path he tried to set out for them, so that the threat of division and disharmony has raised its head. A group of *nouveaux riches* within the Church admire the rhetorically gifted speaker Apollos over the more dull and unexciting Paul (1 Cor. 2.5–9). They feel at liberty to go to dinner parties in pagan temples despite the scruples of other Christians in the Church (8.1–13; 10.7–33). At the Church's common meal, they eat separately from the less well-off and interesting members of

15

the Church (11.17–22, 34), and generally look down on the 'less honourable' members of the community (12.23).

They don't think much of Paul as he is not only a dull speaker, but also a common artisan, working with his hands, not earning a living by his teaching as any respectable philosopher would do (9.1–6). They perhaps ignored or denied the outlandishly counter-cultural idea of resurrection (15.12), perhaps imitating others in more Hellenistic educated circles in Corinth who also disdained such a strange idea (15.32–3). In other words, a significant group in the Church seems to be quite enamoured with the sophisticated ways of the world within the wider city of Corinth. Paul's summary of the focus of their desires was that they looked for 'words of human wisdom' (1.17).

This 'wisdom' was simply the normal way of the world in Corinth. It was a kind of blend between Greek ideas and rhetorical skill. The ideology that lay behind it denied resurrection (Chapter 15), took a fairly hedonistic approach when it came to food and sexual activity (Chapters 5 and 6), and admired the more exotic spiritual gifts

(Chapter 14), perhaps like some of the mystery religions that were common in a city such as Corinth. This group of Corinthian Christians were particularly drawn to Apollos because he had just the gifts that would be admired in a culture that values eloquence, verbal fireworks and clever oratory. Such rhetorical deftness was one of the signs of wisdom in this culture. Isocrates, one of the greats of the Greek rhetorical tradition had identified the link between outward speech and inward wisdom: 'the power to speak well is taken as the surest index of sound understanding and discourse which is true and lawful and just is the outward image of a good and faithful soul.'[1] For this way of thinking, eloquent speech is the sure sign of real wisdom and understanding. Someone incapable of smooth, persuasive rhetoric was not worth listening to, and those who were able to perform dazzling flights of verbal dexterity were the idols of the day.

It seemed that there was a group in the Church at Corinth who had been converted to Christ in name but not in reality. They owned the name of Christ, but scratch a little beneath the surface and

1 Isocrates, *To Nicocles*, 5–9.

little had changed from what they thought and how they behaved beforehand. Paul presumably thought long and hard about how he would respond to the various snippets of news he had received from members of the congregation who were still loyal to him. When he does respond to this complex, and perhaps not unusual pastoral dilemma, he starts his answer by reflecting on the cross of Jesus: 'For the message of the cross is foolishness to those who are perishing, but to us who are being saved it is the power of God' (1 Cor. 1.18).

Like Jesus before the Jewish Sanhedrin, Paul stands before the Greek philosophers and orators. He stands before the whole ethos and culture of educated people, the assumptions they make, the values they hold, the things that seem self-evident and obvious. This new faith was bound to confront the 'wise' of Greek, Hellenistic culture, just as Jesus' trajectory was bound to bring him into conflict with the culture of Jewish Jerusalem.

Crucifixion and the Roman Empire

Paul confronts the philosophers armed with a message that centres on a crucified Jewish labourer. Crucifixion was not just another means of disposing of criminals. It had a particularly political meaning in the Roman imperial machine. Crucifixion was reserved for those the empire wanted to make an example of. In a world terrified of the ever-present possibility of a revolt of the entire class of slaves, who vastly outnumbered their masters, the runaway slave needed to be taught a firm lesson.

Condemned murderers, especially those like Barabbas, who had taken part in an insurrection against the Romans, also needed to be very publicly shamed. Political enemies of the state were likewise liable for this most brutal of ends. Crucifixion was the most public form of death imaginable. Stripped naked, usually beaten as a prelude to the main act of savagery, shorn of all dignity and honour, the victim was nailed, arms spread wide to a cross-beam, with a further nail through the ankle bones, and left to die. Death usually came eventually not through loss of blood or the sheer pain, but through asphyxiation, as each breath involved lifting the body up on the nails to give room in the lungs for an intake of air.

In the end, the effort simply became too much, and the victim suffocated to death.[2]

The point, however, was not so much to inflict pain, but humiliation. This was a way of saying to anyone watching that Roman power is absolute, and it is futile to resist. If you are a slave, a Jewish wannabe rebel, or someone thinking of challenging the power of the emperor, think again – you do not want to end up like this. The Roman Empire was built on such displays of naked power. The empire existed by war against tribes or peoples either yet to be subjected, or already subject but in revolt. It was impossible to aspire to power in the Roman Senate without money, and if you did achieve the status of emperor, you held it largely by fear and bribery until someone else mounted a successful coup to unseat you. This was a system built on power with the cross as a symbol, not of divine love or forgiveness, but of punishment, of pure unadulterated force.

2 For a more detailed analysis of the reality of crucifixion in the first century, see M. Hengel (1977). *Crucifixion*. London, SCM Press.

This, of course, is how Jesus' career had apparently ended. It was not the end his followers or his family expected, especially when they were caught up in the euphoria of the early days of the movement in Galilee, when the dramatic healings, the miraculous stilling of storms and the stunning wisdom of his teaching had made such an impression.

Familiar from many of our childhoods might be an image of three crosses on a 'green hill far away' – a pastoral scene, with perhaps a sunset in the distance, but with three perfectly proportioned crosses perched on a gentle grassy mound. The reality was very different.

The location was most probably a small quarry just near the Gennath Gate of the city of Jerusalem. The walls of today's Old City of Jerusalem take a different route, and the likely site of execution, now marked by the Church of the Holy Sepulchre, lies within the current walls. In the first century, the site lay just outside the city, important for the purpose as Jewish sentiment would have been outraged by executions taking place within the city, and Roman policy, while keeping the Jews in their place, was not to inflame things unnecessarily.

So we are to imagine a desolate scene, a bare stretch of rock which had been left by the earlier stone cutters because it was cracked, which stood out from the rising gradient of the hill, and which provided a convenient location for a set of Roman crosses, clearly visible from the city (important for deterrence) yet judiciously outside the walls themselves. Execution has always fascinated people, has always gathered crowds, some sympathetic to the victims, some decidedly not so. The gospels tell of passers-by hurling insults at him: 'So! You who are going to destroy the temple and build it in three days, come down from the cross and save yourself!' That is probably polite compared to the colourful and angry language actually used. A set of *kokhim* tombs was conveniently located nearby, where corpses could be laid out and left until they had fully decayed, at which time the bones would be collected together and put into ossuaries, small caskets which were then finally buried. It was a place that reeked of death, a place of wretchedness, despair and defeat, a place that emphasized the utter power and implacable might of Rome.

Jesus, contrary to expectation, had allowed himself to be hung, nailed, impaled on this roughly and hurriedly assembled scaffold, amongst the assortment of criminals, rebels and general riff-raff that the Roman occupation in Jerusalem had decided should die that day. For most onlookers there was nothing that suggested that this collection of crucifixions was any different from any other. There were no halos, no doves, no divine glow, just the slow, low groaning of a long-drawn-out, excruciatingly painful death. Crucifixion was the death reserved for failures, for the beaten. And everyone knew it – the cross was a symbol, known throughout the Roman Empire, of death and defeat.

The word of the cross

Perhaps this begins to help us see the startling nature of what Paul does when he confronts the wisdom of Greek philosophy and rhetoric with the 'message of the cross'. Paul suggests that this scene – this unlikely scene of devastation and failure – is the epicentre of power and the wisdom of God. It is the place where God's wisdom is made known, the place where he is most clearly revealed.

To these sophisticated Corinthians, with their social hierarchies, exclusive attitudes and liking for eloquent speakers, Paul says: it just doesn't work like that. You are looking for wisdom? God starts with foolishness. You think the way lies in upward social mobility? God points the way to downward social mobility. You think truth is found in finely crafted words and persuasive, interesting ideas bandied around at dinner parties in pagan temples? God's truth is found in a topic of conversation you would never bring up in such a context: crucifixion.

If ever there was an argument for atheism, the crucifixion of Jesus is it. There are, of course, all kinds of more or less cogent philosophical and cultural arguments mounted by atheists against religious beliefs, but none come with as much force as this. Here is Jesus of Nazareth, supposedly the Son of God, the one who lived entirely according to the will and purpose of God, the one who, if anyone ever did, deserved God's help and intervention. And when he needs divine help and rescue, what happens? Nothing. God (if there is a God) does nothing. Precisely at the place and point at which you would expect God to intervene, there is a deafening silence. The deliverance that Jesus' friends and family longed and presumably prayed for did not happen. God had forsaken him in his hour of need.

And yet precisely here, the scene of God's absence, is, according to Paul, the scene of his revelation. This picture of foolishness, is in fact the place where God's wisdom is decisively revealed. It does not make sense, or at least it does not do so to conventional human wisdom. Paul suggests that wisdom, truth and salvation are not found through intellectual enquiry, the acquisition of fame, rhetorical skill or a life of comfort, ease and affluence, but that this scene of violence, pain and suffering is, somehow, the vital clue to the meaning of life.

This is a scene which any sensible person would run away from, not embrace. And yet, says Paul, true wisdom and understanding starts here, in this deserted quarry with blood dripping onto the naked stone amongst the cries of agony and grief. A crucified, shamed and humiliated man is in fact the wisdom and the revelation of the God who made the universe.

In the early 1500s, while the young Martin Luther was enduring a tough period of questioning his calling, even his salvation, a conversation with Johannes von Staupitz, his superior in the Augustinian Order of friars helped to set him on the right path. Years later, Luther recalled the words Staupitz uttered that shifted things, the piece of advice that started him thinking in a new way. Luther had been somewhat introspective, looking within himself to discern right motives, feelings, virtues. Instead, Staupitz suggested: 'Why do you torture yourself with these speculations? Look at the wounds of Christ.'[3] This, Luther often said, was one of the turning points for him in a process that led to his new theological approach, and in turn led to the great Reformation of the sixteenth century.

Staupitz's advice is similar to that which Paul gives to the Christians in Corinth who are still beguiled by the ways of the world in their city, the norms and expectation that common sense dictates. Paul says to them: look instead at the cross. There, we see a scene which confounds human wisdom, that goes against all our expectations of how we like life to work out, how good people should be treated. Later, Luther would often say that if you want to understand the Christian faith, you

3 Martin Luther, *Works* 5:47.

must begin, not with looking inside yourself, or even speculating on whether or not there is a God and if so, imagining what he might be like, but instead with the cross of Christ. As Luther put it later: 'true theology and recognition of God are in the crucified Christ.'[4]

Luther was saying something very similar to what Paul is suggesting to the Corinthian Christians. We cannot think our way to God through what appears to be just common sense. The Christian way is different from the way of the world. We cannot simply observe the world and reason our way to God, or work out what he might be like. If we did we would end up with what Blaise Pascal later called 'the God of the philosophers'. We would construct an idea of God that is far removed from the true God, a God of our own imagination, a God we can make sense of, a God we can believe in, a God who is smaller than the real God, made in our own image, in other words, an idol.

Some while ago, I picked up a book in a second hand bookshop. It was an old, slightly faded paperback with what looked like an intriguing

4 Martin Luther, *Works* 31:53.

title: *The God I Want*. Published in the late 1960s, it was a collection of essays by various public figures explaining the kind of God they could cope with, the God they could bring themselves to believe in. None of them said they wanted a crucified God. The cross of Jesus simply bars the way to that approach by confronting us with something that so offends common sense that it makes us start back at square one. It directs us, at the start of our search for God to a scene which tells of the absence of God, the strange and counter-intuitive wisdom of God. It tells us that if we are to find the true God, we need to give up our ideas of what God should be like and sit and listen for a while. It tells us that the journey to find God starts, not with human wisdom, human chattering and speculation on what kind of God we might like, what kind of God we can get our heads around, what kind of God we can bring ourselves to believe in, but instead, we should stop talking, just for once. The journey to God begins in silence, not speculation.

One of the basic starting points for a Christian understanding of God is that God is greater than we are. If there is a God who is so much more magnificent, creative and wise than we are, a God who is unfathomable and literally beyond us, what makes us think we could understand him at all, any more than an ant could understand anything of what it is to be a human being? The attempt to imagine God is a foolish enterprise, a venture doomed to failure. It will always end up with a small God, a God that can fit into our tiny minds, a God that we can understand, not a God who understands us.

The only way in which we might begin to understand this God is if in some way he decides to reveal himself to us, if he chooses to slip out from behind the veil that hides him from us most of the time. And when he does, he turns out to be different from what we would expect.

This book is all about learning to look at the world with different eyes. It tries to help us see the world differently, by looking at it through the lens of the cross. Yet the starting point is not so much looking at the world, but trying to make sense of who this God is who made the world. Paul's 'word of the cross' tells us that before we do this we need to throw out all our common-sense notions of who God might be and be willing to start all over again.

We so often try to fit God into our lives and ways of thinking, and he just won't fit. He didn't for the Sanhedrin. He didn't for the sophisticated worldly Christians in Corinth. He won't for us either. We need to start all over again, giving up our cherished ideas of what God should be like. Most people who reject God have an idea of the God they are rejecting. They have some kind of mental image of God that they have decided is not conceivable. There are a few critics of Christianity who have understood exactly what it is they are rejecting when they reject God, but not many. The cross invites us to throw away such notions, all our idolatrous ideas of God and begin again.

What does all that mean? It means not so much understanding the cross as a discrete idea or theory, but learning to look through the cross as this book tries to do. Paul's bold claim was that the cross, which seems utter madness, is in fact the secret of finding true wisdom. This world is one where its Creator once hung on a rough cross erected in its earth. To begin to grasp that, and to learn to see life through the lens of that startling fact, is the beginning of real understanding.

The best theology begins and ends in silence. It begins in silence as we stop our idle chattering and listen to what God has to say. We start by listening for the quiet, strong, deep voice of God speaking to us through the pages of Scripture, through the words of those who have come to know him best through the centuries. It also ends in silence, as when we begin to glimpse the greatness, the mercy, the wisdom of God, there is not much we can say in return, apart from to wonder and worship. In between there may be many words, and this book will contain some of them. There is conversation to be had, questions to ask and ideas to explore, but all the while expecting to be quietened by the presence of God before whom all voices fall silent.

At the end of the book of Job, when God appears to this man who has lost everything and struggled with the question 'why?', after all his arguments and discussions with his 'friends' and counsellors, he says:

> Surely I spoke of things I did not
> understand,
> things too wonderful for me to know.

My ears had heard of you
   but now my eyes have seen you.
Therefore I despise myself
   and repent in dust and ashes.

That is the silence that comes when finally worship and theology blend into one. Our attempt to look at the world through the lens of the cross begins in a perplexing fashion, by asking us to put aside common sense, to be ready to ask new questions and see the world with new eyes. It will end not in complete understanding, but in wonder and worship which finally is the only way in which we can approach God, and the sign of someone who has begun to deal with the real God, the God of Jesus Christ, the crucified God.

2
THE CROSS AND EVIL

At noon, darkness came over the whole
land until three in the afternoon. And
at three in the afternoon Jesus cried
out in a loud voice, "Eloi, Eloi, lema
sabachthani?" (which means "My God,
my God, why have you forsaken me?").
When some of those standing near
heard this, they said, "Listen, he's calling
Elijah." Someone ran, filled a sponge
with wine vinegar, put it on a staff, and
offered it to Jesus to drink. "Now leave
him alone. Let's see if Elijah comes to
take him down," he said. With a loud cry,
Jesus breathed his last. The curtain of
the temple was torn in two from top to
bottom. And when the centurion, who
stood there in front of Jesus, saw how he
died, he said, "Surely this man was the
Son of God!" (Mk 15.33–9)

For what I received I passed on to you
as of first importance: that Christ died

for our sins according to the Scriptures.
(1 Cor. 15.3)

Jesus dies alone. This is an ugly death, not gently slipping away surrounded by loved ones and friends, but a slow lingering end, with taunts of ridicule in his ears. Apart from a few of his female supporters – the women appear to be the only ones brave enough to watch, and even they only do so from a distance – he is abandoned by his friends, allies, even, it seems by God. These are perhaps the most mysterious and perplexing words in all of Scripture: 'My God, My God, why have you forsaken me?'

It is worth pausing for a moment to catch the astonishing nature of these words. The feeling of abandonment is one of the worst human experiences. The child who suddenly realizes they cannot see their mother, the elderly person abandoned by family, friends, neighbours to live a solitary isolated life in front of the TV, the hostage lying in a cell, apparently forgotten by everyone – all these echo our own big fear – that ultimately we will be abandoned, left alone, isolated from all friendship or relationships.

Jesus cries out his sense of abandonment. Why? Jesus had lived a life of absolute obedience to the Father, a life of prayer, faithfulness and love. And what is his reward? To be abandoned at the last. Just when he needs his Father to remain close, he feels the cold wind of dereliction, of desolation. And yet this is not just a tragedy because this particular individual feels God has abandoned him – this is something deeper and more troubling.

As the gospels tell the story of Jesus, the central fact is his intimacy with God his Father. His core identity was that he was the beloved Son of the Father, as the voice at his baptism announced for everyone to hear (Mt. 3.17). The repeated refrain of John's gospel captures this insight: the Son loves the Father and the Father loves the Son. In fact the whole world is a kind of expression of the love between the Father and the Son: Paul's letter to the Colossians says of the Son, that 'All things have been created through him and for him: in him all things hold together' (Col. 1.16–17). The world is created by the Father in and for Christ. At the heart of and before everything that exists, is found this profound and inexpressible love between the Father and the Son.

35

And yet here on the cross, that love and intimacy is fractured, as Jesus cries out his sense of dereliction by God his Father: 'why have you forsaken me?' The love between Father and Son, out of which the creation was birthed, is broken. A deep fissure opens up in the very heart and being of God – the one thing that holds the world together is torn apart. And it leaves the exact question Jesus himself asks on the cross – why?

At the time, the question was misunderstood. Those standing by thought he was calling out for Elijah to come to help him,[1] or just needed some physical relief – maybe a quick anaesthetic mouthful of alcohol will dull the pain and make it bearable. The question is left hanging in the air, and neither Mark nor any of the gospels give any answer to it, other than the testimony of one of the Roman soldiers, who recognized that despite this sense of abandonment, he was still the Son of God. It is not easy to understand. The bemusement of those standing beside the cross that day is a warning for us not to tread too

---

1 There was a contemporary belief in the imminent advent of Elijah to rescue Israel – see Mt. 17.10.

lightly, or jump to too quick conclusions, lest we too misunderstand.

The cross as atonement

When Paul came to answer the question of why Jesus was abandoned by the Father in his hour of need, he answered it with a deceptively simple statement: 'He died for our sins, according to the Scriptures.' This death of Jesus was somehow connected to human sin, our rejection of God and goodness, expressed in every small petty jealousy and hurtful word, the failure to love, ignoring the divine call on our lives.

The early Christians quite quickly began to interpret the death of Christ as something more than the tragic end to a good life. There were two very good reasons why they began to do this. One is that Jesus himself had spoken of his coming death as a kind of sacrifice, in line with the sacrifices described in the Hebrew Scriptures. The disciples knew all about sacrifices, as they were not only described in full bloody detail in Leviticus, but were the whole point of the Temple in Jerusalem – this was the place where sacrifices could be offered – some for thanksgiving, to be sure, but some as an atonement for the sins of the people.

The Passover was a commemorative meal that recalled the sacrificial lambs whose protective blood was daubed on the houses of the Israelites long ago in Egypt, a sign that the 'angel of death' was to pass over those homes – it was a meal celebrating freedom through sacrifice. Jesus chose to eat the Passover with his followers on the eve of his death, and turned it into a new kind of commemorative meal – this time, remembering not the sacrificial lambs sacrificed for the people, but his own sacrificial death, which was about to take place.

This suggests that Jesus thought of his death precisely as a sacrifice in continuity with the whole sacrificial system of Jewish religion – this was a new, complete and full vision of freedom through sacrifice, of which the Passover was just a shadow. Reflecting on that afterwards, along with some of Jesus' earlier enigmatic sayings about his death as a 'ransom for many' (Mk 10.45) was bound to make Jesus' early followers see his death in a different light.

The other factor was of course the Resurrection. If Jesus was raised from death, then that too was bound to make them look back again at this shameful and traumatic death and view it in a new light. This may have been one of many executions in Roman Jerusalem in these troubled years, but if, out of all those crucified, only *this* man had been raised, this was clearly no ordinary death – there must to more to it than meets the eye. As Peter was soon to say speaking to the crowds at Pentecost: 'God has made this Jesus whom you crucified, both Lord and Christ' (Acts 2.36).

But how does the death of Christ eradicate sins? It was far from obvious at the time, hence the various misunderstandings of those standing around the cross on the first Good Friday, We too struggle to understand this. And yet we need to try. If Jesus did die for our sins as St Paul put it, it is still a stretch to see how our small acts of unkindness and our harsh words connect to this gruesome execution outside the walls of first century Jerusalem.

At the centre of the story of the Bible stands a God of love, mercy and goodness. And yet, the world he has made has decided it can make do without him. Humanity, the part of creation chosen to order and care for that creation, has now become its greatest danger, threatening to destroy it with warfare and violence, and now environmental vandalism and weapons of mass devastation. The biggest threat to the stability and survival of the creation (or at least this part of it – we know too little about the rest of the universe to say) is the very species that was charged with the task of nurturing and developing it, coaxing it to its proper fulfilment. And all of this destructiveness stems initially from the turning away of humanity from God. The symbolic story of Adam and Eve turning a blind eye to God in the garden, then turning against each other conveys a profound truth: that we live in a fractured world because of a fracture in relationships at the heart of the universe.

It still seems, however, a difficult step to make from 'sin' to 'evil'. How are hurtful words, a lack of thoughtfulness, a moment of jealousy linked to this cosmic sense of dis-ease, this wound in creation? The answer is because we live in a radically connected world where our actions have repercussions beyond themselves. If we lived in a world where human beings were effectively isolated individuals, randomly generated from nothing, then it might be possible to think of our actions as having limited consequences. A sin I commit against my neighbour might affect them and perhaps me, but no-one else. Yet the world the Bible offers us is nothing like that – it is a world held together at every moment by its Creator, where we are made for fellowship and community and where every act has ramifications far beyond its immediate context.

We get a glimpse of this deep interdependence of all things in the 'butterfly effect', a term coined by the American chaos theorist Edward Lorenz, by which a relatively minor event, such as the flapping of the wings of a butterfly at one particular moment in a particular place can spark off a chain of events which in turn lead to a tornado. A golfer knows the same thing – a minute change of angle in a golf swing can lead to the ball travelling in a radically different and distressing direction!

Tiny factors can lead to huge results. And this is entirely because we live in a connected world. In previous eras in the west, we were perhaps guilty of forgetting our integral relationship, not just with each other, not even just with God, but with the earth itself. As recent thinking on our relationship with the environment reminds us, we do not live in isolation from the planet on which we live – what we do affects the earth, and what happens in the earth affects us. Tsunamis and earthquakes can destroy us. Sunsets and mountain waterfalls can amaze us. At the same time, carbon emissions and toxic waste can destroy the planet, but gardening and conservation can nurture it. Small acts of goodness can lead to remarkable creativity, yet small acts of anger, vanity or cruelty harm not just those they affect directly, but have the potential to damage the whole cosmic order, and beyond that, grieve the one who holds that order together, God the Creator.

The sense that there is a deep wound in creation that needs healing runs throughout the Old Testament. To take one example, in the book of Isaiah, there is a graphic picture of a deeply damaged world, one that sounds familiar and contemporary:

> The earth dries up and withers, the
> heavens languish with the earth. The

earth is defiled by its people; they have
disobeyed the laws, violated the statutes
and broken the everlasting covenant.
Therefore a curse consumes the earth; its
people must bear their guilt. Therefore
earth's inhabitants are burned up, and
very few are left. The new wine dries up
and the vine withers; all the merrymakers
groan. The gaiety of the timbrels is
stilled, the noise of the revellers has
stopped, the joyful harp is silent. No
longer do they drink wine with a song;
the beer is bitter to its drinkers. The
ruined city lies desolate; the entrance to
every house is barred. In the streets they
cry out for wine; all joy turns to gloom,
all gaiety is banished from the earth. The
city is left in ruins, its gate is battered to
pieces. (Isa. 24.4–12)

A little later however, comes a picture of restoration and health:

On this mountain the LORD Almighty
will prepare a feast of rich food for all
peoples, a banquet of aged wine – the
best of meats and the finest of wines. On

43

> this mountain he will destroy the shroud
> that enfolds all peoples, the sheet that
> covers all nations; he will swallow up
> death forever. The Sovereign Lord will
> wipe away the tears from all faces; he will
> remove his people's disgrace from all the
> earth. (Isa. 25.6–8)

How can this change be possible, given the desolation of the chapter before? How can the healing of the wound of creation come about? When something goes wrong, we have a deep and sure instinct that it can only be healed if justice is done. When a person has abused another, stolen or destroyed what belongs to another, or insulted them to the core of their being, then justice is vital if restoration and healing are to emerge. Sure enough, in between these two passages we find exactly that:

> In that day the LORD will punish the
> powers in the heavens above and the
> kings on the earth below. They will be
> herded together like prisoners bound in
> a dungeon; they will be shut up in prison
> and be punished after many days. The
> moon will be dismayed, the sun ashamed;

for the LORD Almighty will reign on
Mount Zion and in Jerusalem, and before
its elders – with great glory.

The transition from desolation to joy can only
come through justice. Those who have perpe-
trated evil must be held to account. The evil that
has disrupted the world cannot simply be ignored
or glossed over: it must be banished, dealt with,
put right. Restoration is possible, but only when
sin is somehow atoned for.

Back in 1989, ninety-six Liverpool football
fans were crushed to death in the Hillsborough
disaster. At the time, blame was laid on the
fans themselves, for being drunk and disorderly,
claims which the fans' families disputed vigor-
ously. No charges were brought. A strong and
enduring sense of dissatisfaction that something
was not right drove the families to seek justice for
those who had died. In 2012, a definitive report
from an independent panel finally concluded that
the deaths were mostly due to multiple failures
by the police, the emergency services and those
who were in charge on the day. Finally, the truth
was revealed and justice became possible. When

something has gone wrong, justice needs to be done and seen to be done.

Ian McEwan's novel *Atonement* examines exactly this same dynamic. The central character, Bryony Tallis, makes a grave mistake as a young child, falsely accusing her sister's boyfriend of rape, a charge that leads through a prison sentence to untold misery and thwarted hopes. The story is of her attempts to atone for this sin, to find forgiveness. Towards the end of the book comes a reminder of her unresolved guilt and her need for atonement:

> All she wanted to do was work then
> bathe then sleep until it was time to work
> again. But it was all useless, she knew.
> Whatever skivvying or humble nursing
> she did, and however well or hard she did
> it … She would never undo the damage.
> She was unforgiveable.[2]

Can such damage be undone? Only, as the title of the novel suggests, through atonement.

2 Ian McEwan, (2002), *Atonement*. Vintage, London. p. 285.

Atonement is of course a central theme in the Old Testament Scriptures with which Jesus was familiar. The Day of Atonement described in Leviticus 16 was an occasion when the priest made sacrifices for the sins of the people. Bulls or goats were sacrificed or sent into desert with sins confessed over them, as a means of dealing with the sins of the nation. Sins needed to be atoned for, and the whole sacrificial system was an elaborate mechanism for ensuring that atonement was provided.

However, even the Temple sacrifices had not ensured Israel's continued survival. The trauma of exile, and the loss of the Temple in which those sacrifices took place had raised a deeper question mark over whether the blood of bulls and goats was enough to atone for sin. Texts such as Psalm 50 and the book of Amos convey the nagging feeling that Temple sacrifices are inadequate: they do not guarantee divine favour.

The prophets interpreted Israel's exile as divine punishment for Israel's desertion of its calling to remain faithful to the one true God. The nation had strayed from its vocation to be a light to the nations, distinct from all the surrounding peoples and religions, keeping alive the message of a God of goodness, mercy and faithfulness in a world whose gods were violent, rapacious and unpredictable. As a result, Israel had lost the divine favour – God had abandoned her, to the great perplexity of the people who felt sure that God would remain close and keep them from harm. The result was exile – the deportation of the people of Israel to the mighty empires of Babylon and Assyria and the destruction of the beloved and sacred temple of Solomon, the symbol of divine presence and favour.

Israel therefore had asked the same question as Jesus did on the cross: 'why have you forsaken me?' The question echoes through the Psalms, Jeremiah and the book of Lamentations. The answer of the prophets was simple and straightforward: God had abandoned them because they had abandoned God. They were now paying, or atoning, for their sins. Isaiah 53, the famous passage that, read with Christian eyes, seems to speak powerfully of the death of Christ, was originally a text referring to Israel, or some representative figure of Israel, who 'bore our suffering', was 'pierced for our transgressions', and 'bore the sin of many, and made intercession for the transgressors.' The exile was a form of atonement for the offences of the people that had not yet fully been paid – the offering was as yet incomplete.

As Jesus reflected on the Israel of his own day, still far from his Father, still in a kind of exile under Roman rule, perhaps he came to the realization that he was called to complete and bear that ultimate abandonment on behalf, not only of the people of Israel, but of the whole human race – that he was to atone for the sins of the world, to take upon himself the consequences of the human mutiny against God. Certainly after his death, his close followers interpreted his death in those terms as a sacrifice for the sins of the world. Jesus was somehow completing Israel's self-offering as atonement for sin. Jesus suffered abandonment by his Father on the cross just as Israel had suffered abandonment by God in the exile. And by doing so he atoned for the sins of the world, not just the sins of Israel.

Jesus our representative
Yet how can Jesus reconcile humans to God? If Jesus was sinless, as Christian orthodoxy has always said, why does he have to die? Does God punish Jesus as an innocent, guiltless third party? Does that not seem immoral and unfair? Only Bryony

Tallis could atone for her own sins, and it makes no sense to suggest that someone else could do it for her. Surely we have to pay for our own sins, and no just or rightly minded court of law would allow a third party to suffer the penalty instead of the person who has committed the crime?

To answer this problem, it is vital to understand that Jesus died *as one of us.* The Christological controversies of the early Church established the insight that Jesus as the divine Son of God was not a *tertium quid* – a 'third thing' or hybrid between humanity and divinity that is neither one nor the other, but he fully shares the same nature as God and fully shares our human nature as well. How this can be, is the subject for another time, but the significance of this insight for our purpose here is this: that Jesus dies as a representative of the human race. Does humanity atone for its own sins? In a sense yes, in our representative, Jesus, the second Adam. If the blame for the wound of creation lies at the feet of humanity, then humanity has atoned for its sins, in the person of Christ, its representative.

St Athanasius in the fourth century writes: 'taking a body like our own, he surrendered his body to death in place of all, and offered it to the Father. This he did out of sheer love for us, so that in his death all might die and the law of death thereby be abolished.'[3] When Christ dies as one of us, there is a sense in which he dies on our behalf: the whole human race, as it were, dies with him, and pays the ultimate price for its sins. As a result, it can be truly said that we have paid the price for our sins in Christ.

At the same time, the insight that Jesus is fully human and divine tells us that Jesus dies both as a representative of the human race, who bears our full nature, but he also dies, in some sense as the second person of the Trinity, that God is not inflicting pain or punishment on an innocent third party, but bears the abandonment within himself. We will explore this complex area further in chapter 5, yet this insight tells us that this is 'God, reconciling the world to himself in Christ' (2 Cor. 5.19), which is why language of 'God punishing Jesus for our sins' can mislead, if is taken to mean God was outside, untouched by the whole exercise, inflicting pain and punishment on his distinct and innocent Son, Jesus.

3 Athanasius. *De Incarnatione*, 2:8.

Here we are on the borders of a deep mystery. The wound of creation is healed by the wounds of Christ. The deep fissure opened up in the created order through deliberate human disengagement from God the source of all life, is healed through Jesus as our representative, atoning for our sins on the cross.

The New Testament uses a number of images to convey the idea that Jesus' death has fundamentally changed the human condition. We find the idea of the reconciliation of enemies (Rom. 5.10; 2 Cor. 5.19). When people fall out over something trivial, a word of simple apology usually sorts out the problem. When something deeper happens, when a precious child is abused, marriage vows are broken, or the love at heart of the universe is betrayed, there is a costly price to pay. In those circumstances, reconciliation is never cheap or easy. Then, forgiveness and reconciliation cost. Trivial offences can be forgotten or excused. Deeper, grave injustices need deeper healing: either I make the other person pay through revenge, or I bear the cost myself through forgiveness, giving up my right to see the other person suffer. Either way, there is a cost. Suffering is always at the heart of true reconciliation, which is a clue to understanding why atonement is necessary. As Peter Kreeft writes:

> Mercy goes beyond justice, it does not undercut it. If I forgive you the hundred dollar debt you owe me, that means I must use one hundred dollars of my own money to pay my creditors. I cannot really make you a hundred dollars richer without making myself hundred dollars poorer. If the debt is objectively real, it must be paid, and if it is my mercy that repays your debt, I must pay it. That is the reason why Christ had to die, why God could not simply say 'forget it'. Instead he said 'forgive it' and that meant that if we did not pay it, he had to himself.[4]

Reconciliation is not the only image used. We find the idea of 'ransom' (Mk 10.45), a price paid to a captor to ensure the release of a captive. There is the notion of a law court, with acquittal pronounced over the guilty (e.g. Rom. 8.33,

4 P. Kreeft (1992). *Back to Virtue*. San Francisco, Ignatius Press. p. 113f.

Col. 2.14) because their penalty has been paid. Yet these are all metaphors, images used to try to convey something which is itself deeply mysterious and beyond description. The Son of God is abandoned by the Father so that we his adopted children might never be. However we try to explain this and how it works, there will always remain an element of mystery and wonder. And this is right and proper. At the end of the day, the only adequate response at the foot of the cross is wonder and worship, as the soldier himself marvelled: 'Surely this man was the Son of God!' You cannot give a lecture at the foot of the cross. Ultimately we fall silent, with the reverence that is due to holy love and mystery.

Self-sacrifice

Why is Jesus' giving up of his own life the centre of history? Because it is the ultimate act of self-sacrifice, self-sacrifice is the essence of love and God is love. For God himself, in the form of his Son, the one who had every right to all power, authority and glory, to give up his life for the rebellious creation in such a degrading and shameful way, is the greatest act of love. Christ undertook the longest journey, from the highest place to the lowest depths. This is why theologians have sometimes made the startling claim that the cross is the clearest of all revelations of God: because it is the deepest act of love, and therefore speaks most powerfully of the nature of the God who is love.

Strangely out of all recent fiction, the Harry Potter novels have perhaps understood this best. As the various stories in the series proceed, Harry Potter becomes aware, and we the readers become aware of his secret – the secret that makes him special, and that enables him finally overcome the forces of evil. On the night of 31 October 1981, Lily Potter had sacrificed her own life in order to protect her infant son from the dark Lord Voldemort. This act of sacrifice was so powerful that it placed Harry under a magical protection, so that when Voldemort tries to kill Harry in turn, the spell backfires, leaving Harry unharmed (save for a scar on his forehead) and Voldemort bodiless. As Dumbledore, the headmaster of Hogwarts, puts it: 'Your mother died to save you. If there is one thing Voldemort cannot understand, it is love. He didn't realize that love as powerful as your mother's for you leaves its own mark. Not a scar, no visible sign … to have been loved so deeply, even though the person who loved us is gone, will give us some protection forever.'

Self-sacrifice is the heart of love which is the heart of God. That is why ultimately, although it looks paradoxical that God should hang on a cross, it is entirely natural. If God is Love (perhaps the central Christian conviction about God) then of course he would find a way to ensure that his beloved of creation is healed, even if that meant his own self-sacrifice. Martin Luther spoke of a 'theology of glory', a theology that assumed it knew all about God – that he was a God of power, might, glory and majesty alone, and who demands obedience and good works. For such a God, the cross makes little sense. The cross only makes sense for a God who is Love and expresses perfectly the nature and heart of such a God. If the cross makes us start all over again in our understanding of God, it teaches us that first and foremost we are dealing with a God full of burning, passionate, relentless love for his creation – a love that will not let us go. Ultimately evil is overcome not by violence but by love – in fact that is the only force in the universe strong enough to defeat evil – it was true then and it is true now.

3
THE CROSS AND POWER

Pilate asked Jesus, "Are you the king
of the Jews?" "You have said so," Jesus
replied. Then Pilate announced to the
chief priests and the crowd, "I find no
basis for a charge against this man.".…
But with loud shouts they insistently
demanded that he be crucified, and their
shouts prevailed. So Pilate decided to
grant their demand. He released the man
who had been thrown into prison for
insurrection and murder, the one they
asked for, and surrendered Jesus to their
will. (Lk. 23.3–4, 23–5)

At another pivotal point of the Passion story, Jesus stands before his accusers again. Only this time it is not the Sanhedrin, but Pilate. If the Sanhedrin represents wisdom, Pilate represents power. Palestine was a fairly minor province of the Roman Empire that had been conquered back in 63 BC by the innocent-faced but sadistic and brutal Roman general Pompey. Since then, Israel, as it had been in many previous eras, was under the control of a foreign power. Pontius Pilate was the Procurator, a Roman official charged with controlling this awkward city Jerusalem, and its strange people, the Jews. He was already hated in Jerusalem for bringing images of Caesar into the city against Jewish law, going against the policy of earlier, more diplomatic Procurators, who had carefully removed such images from their standards to avoid offence. Pilate was not afraid to use harsh and violent methods. During a rebellion of the Samaritans around Mount Gerizim, their own holy place just a little north of Jerusalem, Pilate had ordered the brutal suppression of the uprising, which involved the killing not just of those who fought the Roman cohorts, but also those who were innocently running for shelter and safety.

On another occasion, Pilate's ambitious plan to bring water into the city through an (admittedly remarkable) aqueduct had been completed using 'sacred money', which was not meant for such worldly use, another decision that was never going to endear him to the Jewish people. During the unrest that followed, he ordered his troops to surround the protesting crowds, and at a given signal, draw hidden daggers, killing as many as possible in the chaos. Pilate had power, and was unafraid to use it.

Pilate had undoubted power over Jesus. He literally had the power of life and death over him. While the Sanhedrin could decide against Jesus, as a religious court, they could not execute him. That could only be decided by the ultimate power in Rome, the empire, represented in Jerusalem by Pontius Pilate himself. The fateful decision to condemn or acquit Jesus was his. Yet the story, as it is told in the gospels, reveals a deeper, hidden question – who really holds power here? As Jesus stands before Pilate in the Praetorium, the platform just in front of Herod's Citadel which served as the headquarters of the Roman presence in Palestine, the question hangs in the air: who is the more powerful of these two men? Is it Pilate, the one who holds political, military power? Or is it Jesus who seems to exert a different kind of power altogether? The encounter is unsettling. It begins to question our understanding of how power operates and who really has it. What does power look like, when viewed through the lens of the cross?

Paul and power in Corinth

Moving forward to Corinth, Paul also confronted not just wisdom but power. Back in chapter 1, we looked at the complex dilemmas Paul faced as he tried to coax the new Christian congregation there onwards. The group who were causing the trouble in the Church were among the upwardly-mobile, not the richest or the most aristocratic, but those who aspired to be so.[1] They were those who had tasted some the benefits of worldly power and wanted more. Such power enabled them to see themselves as above the 'ordinary' Christians, as just a little more sophisticated than most of the other Christians there.

The city of Corinth had been re-founded as a Roman colony by Julius Caesar in 44 BC. Without the long aristocratic tradition that longer-established Roman cities held, the room for social mobility was greater here than in many other places. Recently emancipated slaves from elsewhere in the empire were attracted by the prospect of moving up through the heavily

---

1 This is the conclusion reached by S. M. Pogoloff (1992). *Logos and Sophia: The Rhetorical Situation of 1 Corinthians*. Atlanta, Scholars Press. p. 197–212.

stratified society of a community such as Corinth, without the glass ceiling of ancient noble families who occupied all the important positions in civic life, as was the case in more established cities. This group, with a mind-set that betrayed more of the influence of the social expectations of pagan Corinth than the mind of Christ, were most likely those on the up, those who aspired to power and would use the normal means to get it.

As we saw back in Chapter 1, they were not averse to attending dinners in pagan temples, cheerfully eating meat that had been used in pagan worship, despite the fact that this troubled the less exalted members of the congregation (10.27–33). A litigious spirit was abroad, with Christians taking one another to secular courts to get their rights (6.1–11). Upwardly mobile people would often attach themselves to wealthy and influential patrons, and this was exactly the pattern of behaviour replicated in the Church by those who declared their allegiance to Peter, Apollos or even Paul (1.12). They ate apart from the others at the common meal, keeping their distance and privilege intact (11.18–33). Paul's charge against them is that, while they are called to be distinct, they are acting just like everyone else in Corinthian society, sometimes even worse (5.1): 'Are you not worldly? Are you not acting like mere human beings?' (3.3).

When Paul stops to think about what he will write to them, he thinks not so much of power, but of weakness. He reminds the Corinthians who are gathered to read his letter, perhaps in the house of the wealthy but loyal Stephanas (16.15f.), that when the Church was planted, not many of those who came to faith were from particularly noble families or backgrounds, not many held power in the civic life of Corinth. Some were higher up the social scale, for example, Erastus was the city treasurer and Gaius had a large enough home to accommodate the whole Church (Rom. 16.23f.), but most were not. God had seen fit to build the early Corinthian Church not with high-born nobility, not the bright and the beautiful, but with a mixture of slaves, artisans, those who scraped a living in one of the small trades that could be practised in Greco-Roman cities like Corinth, along with just a smattering of the rich and famous. God had chosen the weak, not the powerful, to shame the strong (1.27).

Moreover, God had not only chosen a fairly unimpressive group to make up his chosen people in Corinth, he also chose a fairly unimpressive person as his agent in bringing the gospel of Christ to the Gentiles. Paul reminds them that when he came to Corinth in the first place, he came in 'weakness, great fear and trembling' (2.3). He visited Corinth after his time in Athens, a place where he had seen mixed success (Acts 17.32) and where, as far as we can tell from the New Testament, he was unable to plant a lasting Church, even though a few people became believers after his speech in the Areopagus.

Perhaps he was struggling with his recurrent eye problems; perhaps his comparative failure in Athens had reminded him how poor a rhetorician he was. Writing later to the Corinthian Church, in words which obviously stung him, he reported others' impressions of him: 'in person he is unimpressive, and his speaking amounts to nothing' (2 Cor. 10.10). And yet here in this first letter, he emphasizes his very weakness and lack of gifts: 'my message and my preaching were not with wise and persuasive words, but with a demonstration of God's power, so that your faith might not rest on human wisdom, but on God's power' (2.5).

Paul in Corinth had little status. He did not come with letters of recommendation from notable contacts as many philosophers would do when visiting a strange city, passports to influence in a new setting (2 Cor. 3.1). If anything, he came as a relatively poor artisan, a leather-worker who sewed tents together for a living. Any respectable philosophical teacher visiting a city such as Corinth to promote his philosophy would never stoop to such a menial task, relying instead upon his oratorical skill to attract a wealthy patron and earn a living. Paul's choice, to work in one of the small 'shops' in the main street of Corinth, sewing his sheets of leather while everyone walked by, was clear evidence to everyone that he was just not good enough to cut it. In a culture very conscious of honour and shame, it would be humiliating to have him as your teacher when there were many others on offer, far more able and impressive to listen to, whose lectures and teaching drew enough of a crowd for them to be economically self-sufficient. Paul, the person God had seemingly chosen to bring this message that the way was now open for the Gentiles to become part of God's people, had little 'power', in the conventional sense of that word. He was, quite frankly, something of an embarrassment.

Even more striking than the choice of socially disadvantaged Christians and a rhetorically useless apostle, is God's choice of a crucified messiah as the Saviour of the world. If power is influence, the ability to get things done, to make things happen, to change circumstances and people, how does God achieve the most difficult thing imaginable: the salvation of the world? Answer: through a crucified messiah.

As we have already seen, the cross cuts across our expectations of wisdom. It also cuts across our understanding of power. Instead of a display of might, it offers us a picture of powerlessness. It is hard to imagine a less powerful figure than someone nailed to a cross. Not only does he have no economic, social or political power, he cannot even move. He does not even have the ability to shift his limbs, to rescue himself. He is pinioned, stuck, literally nailed down, utterly powerless to do anything about it. He has no apparent influence whatsoever. He cannot move, he can hardly lift himself to breathe; he can simply hang there and suffer. It is an ultimate picture of powerlessness and weakness.

Just as we saw when looking at wisdom, God overturns our expectations. God's ways are not our ways. If we are to learn them, we have to go back to square one. God's power is revealed at the very point where it seems weakest. With that in mind, we touch again on the startling paradox that Paul offers when he claims that it is in the crucified Christ that we find the real 'power of God and the wisdom of God' (1.24). What we see as a picture of total powerlessness is in fact the place where the power of God is made manifest.

So why does God do it this way? Why does God tend not to start with the intelligent, the powerful, those with influence to make things happen? Surely a better strategy for getting the Jesus movement off the ground in Corinth would have been to build a Church made up primarily of some of the ruling council, with many from aristo-cratic, high-born educated backgrounds – surely they would have more influence to enable the Church to grow and flourish? And again, surely it would have been better to choose someone like Apollos, smooth, gifted and capable, rather than the stumbling, rambling Paul as his chosen agent to bring the message of grace to the Roman Empire?

To all these questions, Paul gives his answer:

> God chose the lowly things of this world
> and the despised things—and the things
> that are not—to nullify the things that
> are, so that no one may boast before him.
> It is because of him that you are in Christ
> Jesus, who has become for us wisdom
> from God—that is, our righteousness,
> holiness and redemption. (1.28–30)

Hidden here are two important perspectives on the way power operates when viewed through the cross.

Equal before God

'So that no-one may boast before him'. Faced with a complex situation where some were using their position to 'boast' that they were somehow more worthy of respect, more deserving of attention than others, Paul draws their attention to the way God usually works. As his choice of

67

socially average people, a sick and dull apostle and a crucified saviour tells, God normally works through 'lowly things' to make the emphatic point that he does not need our skills and talents to do his work. From the beginning of the Bible to the end, God is the one who holds all the power, and any power we hold is derived not owned. As the one true God, the creator, redeemer and finisher of all things, God is the source of all authority in heaven and earth, which paradoxically has now been conferred, not to political or economic rulers, but to the crucified, risen and ascended Christ (Mt. 28.18). Human power counts for nothing before God.

Shakespeare's play, *Measure for Measure* is an exploration of the nature of power and mercy. Isabella, the novice nun, trying to persuade the tyrant Angelo to have mercy on her brother Claudio, utters these famous lines, which capture, perhaps better than any other, the ridiculous nature of human authority when it becomes absolute:

> … man, proud man,
> Drest in a little brief authority,
> Most ignorant of what he's most assured,

His glassy essence, like an angry ape,
Plays such fantastic tricks before high
  heaven
As make the angels weep.

Authority or power is something with which we are briefly clothed, but God laughs when we take it too seriously. To be powerless is something we all fear, so we anxiously remind ourselves of all our virtues and capabilities. Our instinct as human beings is to build our sense of worth, our self-confidence and value on our past achievements, looks, wealth, status, job or family. In other words to build it upon something for which we can claim credit, some power or ability that we possess. We tend to come before God dressed in our acquired prowess, our moral victories or life's successes. Yet before God, none of these counts for anything. The truth is that we do not do God a favour by signing up to his cause.

The cross, this paradoxical manifestation of divine contrariness, renders human power empty, because it tells us that the only way we may approach God is through the narrow cross-shaped gate of repentance and faith in the one who died for us. To bring before God our skills, virtues or

69

intelligence, expecting him to be impressed by them, makes the angels weep at our folly.

We are used to stressing the dignity of each person before God, that each person is of value before him. And rightly so – this is that 'exalting the humble and meek' that the *Magnificat* speaks of. At the same time however we need to stress the emptiness of each person before God – the 'bringing down the mighty from their seat'. Our sins and failures do not count before God. But neither do our achievements and successes. Before God, each of us stands naked and defenceless.

This is a truly radical insight. The idea that all people, whether noble, common, wealthy, poor, influential or insignificant have equal standing in the ultimate scheme of things, because they are of equal standing before God is a far-reaching idea that stands at the root of all ideas of human rights, democracy or social equality. And it is a fundamentally Judaeo-Christian idea.

The classical world into which Christianity was born was deeply hierarchical. Plato's ideal Republic had slaves set apart to do all the menial drudgery, and Aristotle simply thought some were just born to slavery. Roman emperors were the possessors of absolute power, able to do exactly as they pleased, until the next pretender to the imperial throne managed to raise a coup, replacing one despot with another.

These were not elected officials accountable to the populace or to God, but were potentates, wielding authority which recognized no rival. The early Christians were accused of being social revolutionaries, not because their churches were full of the poor and disenfranchised, but because they were mixed and indiscriminate – a slave could sit alongside a master, drinking from the same Communion cup, listening to the same teaching as if equally capable of responding to it and worthy to hear it, because both were equal before God. Greeks, Scythians, barbarians, Parthians, all the ethnic minorities in the Roman Empire could meet on a level playing field, with the distinctions between them neutralized by their being 'in Christ' together (Col. 3.11).

When we look through the lens of the cross, human pretensions to power and authority look very different. They look temporary and transient, brief episodes which make not the slightest difference to a person's true worth.

Sometimes this is a hard lesson to learn. We are sometimes so taken with our own achievements and status that we find it hard to believe others aren't. It can be disconcerting to meet someone who is frankly unimpressed by our importance or social standing. Sometimes it is only by having these taken from us that the lesson is truly learnt. That is why the experience of shame and disgrace has often been the most severe and searching tutor in teaching humility. Sometimes God has to break up the faulty and cracked foundations of our lives that might one day bring the house crashing around our ears, in order to lay more lasting, stronger ones.

The power to love

Jesus on the cross may look powerless. Yet it is not quite that simple. As we have seen, when he stands before Pilate, he does in fact display a quite remarkable power over the Roman governor of Palestine. It is the power to be true to his ultimate calling, the power to sacrifice himself for the sake of others.

The cross has always elicited a degree of wonder. How could Jesus have gone through with such physical agony when he didn't have to? How could he have endured the spiritual dislocation to the intimacy with God his Father that was his normal experience? Reading the stories of the early Christian martyrs, or even contemporary ones in places from Iran to Sudan makes us ask the same question. How did they undergo such torture and pain, apparently relishing it, even? In an age where we aspire to comfort, ease and prosperity, what gives someone the ability to endure suffering for the sake of Christ? This is a kind of heroism that is beyond most of us – a power that most of us do not have.

On a more mundane level, what enables someone to live a life of pure dedication and self-sacrifice to others? How can someone devote themselves over years to the welfare of an elderly relative, or a disabled spouse, or a group of troubled young people? That is a kind of 'power' or ability that is quite remarkable, much more so than the kind of power that is evidenced by wealth, or position. Anyone can use the power of money or political authority to further their own interests, or those of their tribe or family – that kind of power is depressingly familiar in our world, and leads to tyranny and oppression. The ability to put aside personal gain or advantage, to seek the good of others before yourself, to forego privilege and comfort is no mean achievement.

In the early years of the twentieth century, Albert Schweitzer was a well-known author of a ground-breaking work in New Testament studies. He was a rising star in the academic world destined, it seemed, for a distinguished career in the top universities of Europe, showered with all the prizes and honours that such a career would bring. In 1905 he shocked the academic world of his time by announcing that he was to give up his promising academic career to train as a doctor, with the intention of working in equatorial Africa. Later, he recalled the unexpected opposition he faced in carrying out his plan:

> My relatives and friends all joined in
> expostulating with me on the folly of my
> enterprise. I was a man, they said, who
> was burying the talent entrusted to him
> and wanted to work with false currency.
> Work among savages I ought to leave
> to those who would not thereby be

compelled to leave gifts and acquirements
in science and art unused.[2]

He found himself accused of conceit, of romantic
disappointment, of professional frustration at the
slowness of his career progression, even though
his was a career which had already brought him
more recognition at the age of twenty-nine than
most academics ever achieve. His action went so
much against the grain that his contemporaries
found it almost impossible to understand. To give
up privilege for the sake of other people is not
to be taken for granted. It is indeed a power, a
remarkable ability. That is the kind of self-sacrifice
that is beyond most of us, while operating out of
our normal ways of thinking. Schweitzer found the
inspiration for this choice in his own deeply help
Christian faith, nurtured by long study of the New
Testament and fascination with the figure of Jesus.

This crucified rabbi, strung up with common
criminals whose guilt was indisputable, is
described by Paul in quite remarkable language:
'Christ Jesus, who has become for us wisdom

2 A. Schweitzer (1933). *Out of My Life and Thought*.
Woking, Unwin. p. 108.

from God – that is, our righteousness, holiness and redemption.' The result of the death of Christ is that we are mysteriously united with him in that death (Rom. 6.5) so that we take on his 'righteousness, holiness and redemption', or his goodness, purity and liberty. As we have seen in the last chapter, he died so that we might live. He sacrificed himself on behalf of a rebellious humanity, that our debt might be paid.

The voluntary submission of God in Christ to a gruesome, violent death on behalf of a human race that had turned away from him in arrogance, is an astonishing act of self-giving, the more so because it is so undeserved. As Paul put it elsewhere:

> Very rarely will anyone die for a righteous
> person, though for a good person
> someone might possibly dare to die. But
> God demonstrates his own love for us in
> this: While we were still sinners, Christ
> died for us. (Rom. 5.7–8)

This is the power of God: the power to go to a cross for people who do not deserve it. It is the power to love.

These two insights into a Christian understanding of power are linked. When a person grasps in a quite profound way, that neither their achievements nor their mistakes count before God, it leaves that person with nothing to lose. And it is so often the fear of loss that holds us back from serving others. Fearing the loss of opportunity, comfort or security, we hold onto what we have, afraid to let it go for the sake of someone else, and so the opportunities for small or large acts of love and compassion slip past us daily. When we learn to 'boast in the Lord' (1 Cor. 1.31), to take our delight not in any quality or gifts that we may possess, but instead in the God who loved us in Christ, the God who, in the person of his Son, died for us, then we start to become capable of similar acts of love. When we have little to lose, we start to give. When we lose the love of power for its own sake, we discover the power to love.

If power is the ability to get things done, to change circumstances and people, then this takes us to the heart of the Christian understanding of power: it is the power of self-sacrificial love and service. There is nothing more powerful than this. Love can soften the hardest of hearts, the most rigid minds, the stoniest of souls. Love can do what naked force cannot. When we are loved we are able to change. When we are unloved we dig in our heels and refuse to budge. Love is the most powerful force in the world. And it is on the cross that we see the most dramatic, powerful and profound act of love: the love of God that voluntarily took all human shame and failure onto himself in the person of his Son. As John puts it: 'This is love: not that we loved God, but that he loved us and sent his Son as an atoning sacrifice for our sins' (1 Jn 4.10). The cross shows us love, and by doing so, shows us a completely new perspective on power: the power of self-sacrificial love to save and to change the world.

4
THE CROSS AND IDENTITY

They compelled a passer-by, who was
coming from the country, to carry his
cross; it was Simon of Cyrene, the father
of Alexander and Rufus. (Mk 15.21)

I have been crucified with Christ and I
no longer live, but Christ lives in me. The
life I now live in the body, I live by faith
in the Son of God, who loved me and
gave himself for me. (Gal. 2.20)

There are times in our lives where we are fairly
confident about our identity. We know who
we are, what we do, where we live and who our
friends are. There are other times in our lives
where we find ourselves dislocated from the
places and people we've been used to, the fixed
points that positioned us in the world, and we
wonder 'who am I now?' Am I this person that I
have been or am I someone new? What is it that
defines 'me'? Is my identity something hidden
deep within me to be discovered? Or is it yet to

be created, waiting to be made? Who am I and where do I fit within the world?

It used to be the case that questions of identity were rarely acute. Identity was fixed by things like family, class, or where a person lived. Now, things are different. Social and geographical mobility mean that the social station someone is born into no longer necessarily defines who they are. There was a time when *nationality* gave people a clear sense of identity. Now that is less likely to be true, with immigration bringing a blurring of national identities, and the distinctives between nations being eroded in a world where every country has McDonalds, Apple and Coke. Nationalism is now likely to be seen, not as an innocent love of country as it once was, but the source of conflict or oppression of one group by another.

Racial origins once gave a strong sense of identity and in some cases they still do, but in a world which lives under the spectre of the Holocaust and the shadow of racism, we feel less at ease about defining ourselves (much less others) purely by race or racial characteristics. *Religion*, or perhaps denominational allegiance, once gave people a sense of personal distinctiveness, yet with the erosion of the influence of faith in public life, not to mention the blurring of religious particularity that emerges from the pluralistic approach that modern societies tend to take towards religions, religious identity is weaker that it used to be.

Gender was once a clear marker of identity – you were either a man or a woman. Now however, with interchangeability of fashion between male and female styles, and the increasing acceptability of various sexual identities means that what were once distinct lines and definitions are now much more blurred and indistinct. *Career* once gave a sense of who people were in the world. You were an accountant, a lawyer, or a bus driver for life. Now, in a world where, during their working life, it is estimated that the average graduate will change jobs eleven times, and their entire skill base three times over, careers are much more flexible, and hence give a less sure sense of identity than before.

Identity is therefore a much more fluid thing than it was, and a source of greater anxiety than it was in a world where the boundaries were more fixed. We now have greater choice, greater opportunities for mobility and change. All that is good, yet the downside is what Alain de Botton called 'Status Anxiety', an uncertainty over where we fit within the natural hierarchies of social life, and a resulting lack of confidence in who we really are.[1]

The result (or perhaps the origins) of this, is what the philosopher Charles Taylor calls the 'subjective turn' in modern culture.[2] No longer sure of who we are, because the external boundaries have shifted, we look not outside ourselves, to a fixed social order, or to God, to tell us who we are in the grand scheme of things, but we look inside to find our true selves. We try to find out who we really are by looking inside ourselves, to some irreducible core that lies within. Our identity is 'given'; we just have to discover it. And when we do, the great moral imperative is to be true to who we really are.

1 A. de Botton (2004). *Status Anxiety*. London, Hamish Hamilton.
2 C. Taylor (1989). *Sources of the Self: The Making of the Modern Identity*. Cambridge: Cambridge University Press and C. Taylor (1991). *The Ethics of Authenticity*. Cambridge, MA: London, Harvard University Press.

Self-expression thus becomes vital. We feel a need to express our inner selves through adopting certain identities, expressed through our choice of clothes, hairstyle, makeup, or style. A consumerist economy is ideally poised to provide just the variety of 'looks' that we might choose. It is also designed so that we can change that look as often as we feel a need to change our identity.

As the sociologist David Lyon puts it, 'postmodern consumers constantly "try on" not only new clothes, new perfumes, but new identities, fresh personalities, different partners.'[3] Sociologists and philosophers speak now of 'the plastic self': identity as something not fixed, but malleable, something that can be moulded into different shapes, time and time again. We can shift from one persona to another with the shifting sands of fashion or mood.

The psychologist Erik Erikson coined the term 'identity crisis' to describe a process through which people, particularly teenagers, undergo a confusion of identity before finding one part of

3 D. Lyon (2000). *Jesus in Disneyland*. Cambridge, Polity. p. 79.

their identity on which they can, at least in part, settle. However, increasing numbers of people now seem to experience a continual identity crisis that never quite seems to settle on anything.

What is a Christian understanding of identity? And more particularly, how do questions of identity look when viewed through the lens of the cross? Can the cross of Jesus help us find a new approach to identity, help us discover new selves?

A visitor surprised

Simon was in Jerusalem for the Passover. He hailed originally from North Africa, from the town of Cyrene in the region which is now Libya. Why was he in the holy city that day? No-one knows for sure, but there are some clues. Had he settled somewhere else in Roman Palestine and come in 'from the country' to visit the city at this key weekend of the year? Cyrene was a Greek colony within the Roman Empire which had a strong Jewish population, so most likely he was a Jew visiting the city for the feast, as many Jews wanted to do, wherever there were in the world. Either way, he could hardly have suspected what was about to happen to him.

Candidates for crucifixion were normally made to carry the transverse crossbeam to the place of execution, where it would then be nailed to the victim's arms and hoisted onto the upright stake that was fixed into the ground and regularly re-used for the gory business of crucifixion. Jesus, weakened by being beaten and whipped, following closely after the emotional agony of the Gethsemane experience, is too exhausted to carry the crossbeam. Wanting to ensure Jesus does not die before he is crucified as a public deterrent to others, the soldiers guarding him look around to find someone standing by whom they can force to carry it to the end of its journey.

Jesus' disciples, of course, are nowhere to be seen. In the wrong place at the wrong time, perhaps drawn along by the fascination of large crowds to scenes of violence, Simon finds himself press-ganged into hauling the cross of Jesus of Nazareth, dangerously close to getting caught up in the execution itself. Simon cannot have carried the cross for very long – it was not a lengthy journey from Pilate's headquarters to Golgotha, just outside the wall of the city – but enough to seal his place in history.

This is the only place Simon is mentioned in the New Testament. It is the only place he is mentioned anywhere. Yet the name of Simon of Cyrene is now known across the world wherever Christians meet and re-tell the story of the crucifixion each Easter, all because of this chance encounter that probably only lasted a few minutes on a violent, tense afternoon during Passover weekend in Jerusalem.

Simon the Christian?

The only other biographical detail we know about Simon is that he was the 'father of Alexander and Rufus'. The comment is made as if Mark's readers will know exactly who he means. Many have suggested this indicates that Alexander and Rufus were members of the Church in Rome, where Mark's gospel was most likely written. They might have nodded knowingly as the story was read out in their presence. Perhaps the Rufus mentioned in Paul's letter to the Romans (16.13) was this son of Simon. His mother (Simon's wife?) also gets a brief mention there as someone who had been something of a mother to Paul too – if this is the same Rufus, this was a strong Christian family which had played a key part in building the young community of Jesus-followers in Rome itself.

Whether or not this is Rufus the son of Simon, if the two sons had become followers of Jesus, then it is most probably because their father had done so before them. This brief encounter had changed Simon's life forever. From being a fairly anonymous Jew, just visiting the city for the festival, through this traumatic episode, he has now become a different person. Who knows how he later reflected on his brief involvement with the story of Jesus?

His close brush with the cross appears to have had such a profound effect on him, that he was never quite the same again. The whole landscape and direction of his life had changed so that he is now a new person, with a new significance and focus for his life. His unintentional identification with the cross of Jesus had transformed him and his family into something different, with a new direction, purpose and identity.

Crucified with Christ

Simon carried the cross on that fateful day. Is there a conscious recollection here of Jesus' words to his followers: 'whoever does not carry their cross and follow me cannot be my disciple'? There were only two people who carried this particular cross: Jesus and Simon. Yet St Paul uses this metaphor to explore in greater depth the meaning of our connection with the cross of Jesus, and how it gives us a new identity, as it did for Simon.

Writing to the Galatian Christians around twenty years after the events of the first Good Friday, he tells them that that he now believes that he, like Simon but in a different way, is intimately identified with the cross of Jesus: 'I have been crucified with Christ and I no longer live, but Christ lives in me. The life I now live in the body, I live by faith in the Son of God, who loved me and gave himself for me' (Gal. 2.20).

Paul has in some way been crucified along with Christ; the person who now lives in his body is no longer the old Paul, but that instead Christ lives now in him. The death of Christ on the cross is no longer a historical event, distant from him in time and space, but he is in a very profound way partnered with Christ on the cross, crucified with him. His old self has died, and a new self has been born.

Just as Christ identifies with us as our representative, we are to identify with him as those 'crucified with Christ'. If Jesus dies as one of us, then we are included in that insofar as we are one with him. We sometimes hear the Christian message explained as that 'Jesus dies so we might live', or 'Jesus died so that we can go free', as if in some way we are not involved in the suffering of Christ. The New Testament writers don't seem to see it quite that way.

The letter of 1 Peter puts it like this: 'He himself bore our sins in his body on the cross, so that we might *die* to sins and live for righteousness; by his wounds you have been healed.' In other words, he died, not so much that we might live, but that we might die – to sin. Similarly, St Paul writes that 'we are heirs – heirs of God and co-heirs with Christ, *if indeed we share in his sufferings* in order that we may also share in his glory' (Rom. 8.17). He also writes of how 'I want to know Christ – yes, to know the power of his resurrection and *participation in his sufferings*, becoming like him in his death, and so, somehow, attaining to the resurrection from the dead.' Our response to the suffering of Christ is to 'offer your bodies as a living sacrifice, holy and pleasing to God'

(Rom. 12.1). In all these texts we find this central theme of identifying with Christ's sufferings, being crucified with Christ, as Paul puts it.

This was expressed for Paul in the fact that he literally did start using a new name after his conversion. In Acts, particularly before his conversion, he is normally called Saul, but later on he starts to use the name Paul. The reasons for this are a little obscure, but perhaps the best explanation is that his real name was Saul (a Jewish name, therefore more likely to be the original one) but that when he began his work as Christian missionary among Gentiles, he adopted the Latinized form of his name, or at least the closest-sounded Latin equivalent, Paul.[4] Either way, it is clear that his identity had fundamentally changed because of the cross of Christ.

Baptism: a new start and a new identity

Paul makes an explicit link between baptism and the cross of Jesus in Rom. 6:

---

4 See J. Murphy-O'Connor (1996). *Paul: A Critical Life*. Oxford: Oxford University Press. pp. 41–3 for a discussion of the possibilities.

Do you not know that all of us who were
baptized into Christ Jesus were baptized
into his death? We were therefore buried
with him through baptism into death in
order that, just as Christ was raised from
the dead through the glory of the Father,
we too may live a new life. If we have
been united with him in a death like his,
we will certainly also be united with him
in a resurrection like his. For we know
that our old self was crucified with him so
that the body ruled by sin might be done
away with, that we should no longer be
slaves to sin – because anyone who has
died has been set free from sin. Now if
we died with Christ, we believe that we
will also live with him.

To be baptized is to be immersed into the death
of Jesus. It is, in some way, to be crucified with
him, so that our old self dies and a new one is
born. The symbolism of baptism is that a person
descends into the waters of death, just as Israel,
escaping from Egypt, passed through the waters
of the Red Sea, and just as Jesus descended to
the realm of the dead. The new Christian then
rises out of the water again, just as Israel emerged

from the waters into the Promised Land, and as Jesus himself rose from the depths of death. A new person is born – the old has gone, and the new has come.

Perhaps our customary image of a family christening – a family gathered around a font, smiling fondly while water is splashed onto the baby's head – somehow fails to capture this radical new event, this urgent and profound break with the past and the forging of a new identity. Yet even here, traces of the true meaning of baptism remain. In churches that perform infant baptism, a child is given a new name, a *Christian* name. Their surname is already decided before birth, coming from the family the child was born into, giving their identity as a member of that family with all its history and particularity. Their *Christian* name however is unique to the child – it is a new name conferred in baptism itself, and the linking of baptism and naming is theologically significant. When we are baptized, entering formally into the family of God, we take on a new identity, a new name – we are a new person. In the Middle Ages, babies were often given the name of the saint on whose day they were baptized.

For example, Hans and Margarethe Luther gave their son the name Martin because he was baptized on 11 November, the day after he was born in 1483, which was (and is) St Martin's day. In many non-Christian cultures around the world, when adults are baptized into the Christian Church they are given new, distinctly Christian names, which identity them as Christians to their neighbours, friends and family. It is not just that Christians should be new people, they are new people. Their baptism into the death of Jesus means a new identity. The old self dies as she is lowered under the water; her new Christian self rises as she emerges alive again from the water to a new world.

Even more than this, it means renewing our sense of identity day by day. Martin Luther once wrote: 'Thus a Christian life is nothing else than a daily baptism, begun once and continuing ever after. For we must keep at it without ceasing, always purging whatever pertains to the old Adam, so that whatever belongs to the new creature may come forth.'[5] Every day, we are to go back to our

5   The Large Catechism (Book of Concord p. 445).

baptism, reminding ourselves of who we really are in Christ, our new selves.

In the early Church, testimony before others was a vital part of Christian witness. The Greek word for witness *marturion*, is the word from which we gain the word 'martyr'. One of the earliest and best known Christian witness/martyrs was Polycarp, bishop of Smyrna who was executed under the emperor Marcus Aurelius in 155 AD. When pressed during his trial, he uttered the bold and remarkable words: 'if you pretend not to know who I am, I will tell you plainly: I am a Christian.'[6] Here was someone who knew exactly what he was: his primary identity was not a native of Smyrna, or even a bishop in the Church: it was, quite simply and plainly, a Christian.

If the cross is to benefit us, if we are to find the forgiveness, the new life that we have explored so far in this book, then it will mean for us, as it did for Simon of Cyrene, for Saul of Tarsus, and for Polycarp, a new identity. It will mean a kind of death, not just for Christ, but in a way for us

6 Eusebius (1965). *The History of the Church*. London, Penguin. p. 171.

as well. That old self, defined by my family, social status, educational background or achievement, class or race will die and a new Christian self will be born.

So often as we have seen, those old identities are the source of so much conflict in our world. To define myself by my race, or nation, job or class is to define myself over against others, to place myself in opposition to them. Of course there is a way of using 'Christian' identity in the same way. When 'Christian' just becomes a badge for a tribe, a religion just like any other religion, it can become as much a source of conflict as any other name or cultural label.

If our new Christian identity is forged in the cross, then that identity can never be a way of separating myself from others, placing myself over *against* the 'ungodly', but instead an identity which invites me to be *for* them, just as Jesus died *for* the ungodly (Rom. 5.6). A new identity that emerges from identification with Jesus on the cross is one that places me in the same relation to others as the crucified Jesus has: called to offer myself for the good of others, to that same self-sacrificial love displayed on the cross. If the cross

points us to a God whose most essential characteristic is love, then our new identities are bound
up in that same God – we are to be re-made
around love, re-defined as those called to a life of
love and self-giving.

It means that the old identity markers, the ones
that cause so much grief and division in our world,
no longer define us. I am no longer defined by
my job, my family, my nation or my tribe, but by
Christ. Christian identity is not found by turning
within, to find my true self, as if it lies hidden
within waiting to be discovered, but instead it
is found by looking outside myself to Christ –
becoming Christ-like, capable of self-sacrificial
love, in my own distinctive way. Writing to the
Christians in Colossae, Paul expressed this same
idea of being reborn in Christ 'For you died, and
your life is now hidden with Christ in God. When
Christ, who is your life, appears, then you also will
appear with him in glory' (Col. 3.3–4). Our true
selves are found not hidden in some secret place
within ourselves, but are found outside ourselves,
in Christ. In a sense, who I truly am is yet to be
seen, yet to be revealed. It is being built even
now as I grow in likeness to Christ, one day to
be revealed 'when Christ, who is my life appears.'

The new and the old self

People take on new identities in different ways in our culture. There is now a new kind of crime, called 'identity theft' where someone can steal another person's identity by getting hold of their credit card number, passport, computer login details. If they can get these basic details, they can basically take over a person's entire identity. As a result the victim can find themselves stranded, with a question mark over their very existence – if someone else has your name, your bank details and your online profile, they can take over who you are, leaving you in limbo, struggling to convince others you are who you say you are.

On other occasions, we hear of witnesses to a crime or juvenile offenders who are given a new identity. For their own safety, they are given a new name, a new home, a new role. No one knows who they are, as they start all over again. They have to somehow try to live out this new identity they have been given, as if they are no longer the person they once were, the one that got them into trouble in the first place, but instead are this new person with a new name, a new role, a new home, new job – in fact with everything being new.

This phenomenon of changed identity is often difficult. In one recent case of a young offender who was given a new identity after completing his custodial sentence, a consultant forensic psychiatrist commented: 'Double lives are a burden for people. Juggling two identities is stressful and the secrecy takes its toll. People are not necessarily well-equipped to do this sort of thing. It's not their natural state.'

It is often hard to live with two identities – the old person and the new – and it is apparently quite common for people in this situation to feel compelled to tell others who they were, to reveal their past identity, to go back to the old self, to somehow live out of who they were, not what they had become.

This picture of taking on a new identity perhaps helps us understand what Paul means when he talks about being crucified with Christ. When he was met by Christ in that dramatic encounter on the Damascus road, and was subsequently baptized into Christ, the old Saul died. That 'old Saul' was an academic, a scholar and religious conservative who came from an important family in Judaism. He was proud of his ancestry, full of animosity towards people who were different from or beneath him. But when he was baptized it is as if that person died and a new person was born. And for him it actually was embodied in a new name. Saul of Tarsus became Paul the Christian. Here was a new person, forgiven, free, oriented entirely towards the Son of God 'who loved me and gave himself for me' as he later put it. His identification with the cross of Jesus created in him a person with a new identity.

Just like the young offender given a new identity, Paul too still felt the pull of the old one. Later in the same passage in Colossians mentioned above, Paul writes: 'You have taken off your old self with its practices and have put on the new self, which is being renewed in knowledge in the image of its Creator. Here there is no Gentile or Jew, circumcised or uncircumcised, barbarian, Scythian, slave or free, but Christ is all, and is in all.' The old self has been put, off like an old coat, and a new one put on. His task is to try to live out of this new identity, the new self. That is the invitation we are given from the cross of Christ: to start to live out this new identity we have in Christ: redeemed, forgiven, loved, blessed and called to give ourselves for the sake of those God has placed around us in often small and mundane, but occasionally large and painful ways. It is to live out who we truly are in Christ.

We still constantly feel the pull of the old self, the insecure, needy, nagging self, always wanting to be pleased and satisfied. But we will not always feel its drag upon us. Towards the end of C. S. Lewis's book *The Pilgrim's Regress*, a traveller and his guide come to a stream. The traveller says to the guide, 'This stream looks, somehow, vaguely familiar.' The guide replies, 'That's right. We call this brook "death". It's too tough a morsel to eat at one bite. You will meet this brook more often than you think and each time you'll suppose that you've done with it for good, but someday you really will.'[7]

One day we will no longer feel the pull of the old self, and will be transformed fully into the new person Christ had invited us to be. A Christian is a new person with a new name, defined not by mistakes made nor by achievements gathered, but by Christ, by a new Christian self, defined by

7 C. S. Lewis (1977). *The Pilgrim's Regress*, Glasgow: Fount, p. 220.

the call to love. 'I have been crucified with Christ and I no longer live, but Christ lives in me. The life I live I live by faith in the Son of God who loved me and gave himself for me.' And that is the invitation of Good Friday: to live as new people defined not by the past, but by the future. Defined not by what we have been, but by what we will one day become: restored, redeemed, fully remade in Christ.

5

THE CROSS AND SUFFERING

Who has believed our message? And to
whom has the arm of the Lord been
revealed? He grew up before him like a
tender shoot, and like a root out of dry
ground. He had no beauty or majesty
to attract us to him, nothing in his
appearance that we should desire him.
He was despised and rejected by others,
a man of suffering and familiar with pain.
Like one from whom people hide their
faces, he was despised and we held him in
low esteem. (Isa. 53:1–3)

Then he called the crowd to him, along
with his disciples and said: "Whoever
wants to be my disciple must deny
themselves and take up their cross and
follow me. For whoever wants to save
their life will lose it, but whoever loses his
life for me and for the gospel will save it.
(Mk 8.34–5)

Alex McCandless was a young man from a well-off family who chose to abandon all the trappings of modern life, to hitchhike alone into the Alaskan wilderness to live off the land, a radically different life from the money- and ambition-fuelled path trodden by most of his contemporaries. In his early journeys away from civilization, he met a man called Ronald Franz, who was at the time a devout Christian. Franz had spent most of his life in the US Army, stationed in the Far East. On New Year's Eve 1957, his wife and child had been killed by a drunk driver in a car accident. He hit the bottle hard, but still went to church, hanging in there with his faith. When he met McCandless, his paternal instincts re-emerged, as he was struck by this young man's intensity, focus and joy in life. After they had become friends, McCandless continued his journey into the wilds of Alaska, only to die there of starvation, alone and isolated. When Franz heard the tragic story of his young friend's death, he wrote:

> When Alex left for Alaska, I prayed. I asked God to keep his finger on the shoulder of that one; I told him that boy was special. But he let Alex die. So

on December 26th when I learned what
had happened, I renounced the Lord.
I withdrew my church membership
and became an atheist. I decided I
couldn't believe in a God who would let
something that terrible happen to a boy
like Alex.[1]

It is a story that has been told many times. Many
former Christians are believers no more because
something happened that made them think 'How
could a loving God allow that to happen?' Others
who are decidedly not Christians choose not to
believe for very similar reasons, struggling to
see how a good God could allow such dreadful
things to happen to good people in his world.
The problem of suffering is one of the major
obstacles to faith for countless people in the
modern world, and an area of doubt and vulner-
ability for many who would describe themselves
as committed faithful Christians.

The philosopher Epicurus in the third century
BC famously formulated the problem of evil thus:

1 J. Krakauer (1996). *Into the Wild*. New York: Pan Books.
   p. 61.

> Is God willing to prevent evil, but not
> able? Then he is not omnipotent. Is
> he able, but not willing? Then he is
> malevolent. Is he both able and willing?
> Then where does evil come from? Is he
> neither able nor willing? Then why call
> him God?

The result of this argument was a basic form
of soft hedonistic atheism. Epicureans doubted
the gods were at all interested in life on earth,
if they existed at all. If the gods don't care, or
don't exist, then we might as well enjoy the few
days we have here of this bleak existence – a very
common attitude in the modern world. Many
ordinary contemporary people are Epicureans
without knowing it.

Atheism in the ancient world however was
relatively rare. Alister McGrath recounts how
'the problem of suffering' as we call it was not
so much of a problem for Christians before the
eighteenth century.[2] Before that time there are
almost no references to this objection being

2 A. McGrath (1992). *Bridge-Building: Effective Christian
   Apologetics.* Leicester: IVP. p. 139f.

raised as a reason for not believing in God. Of course the awareness of suffering and its relation to God are not new – the book of Job is one Old Testament text that acutely addresses that issue. It brings into question the goodness of God, yet it never occurs to Job to doubt his existence.

Perhaps in the past there was a more general acceptance of suffering as an inevitable part of life; now, we are more used to a comfortable existence where it is possible to keep suffering at a distance for a while, and when it does intrude onto our horizon it can come as a shock, disturbing our rosy view of the world. Perhaps our ability to reduce suffering in the world through modern medicine and technology makes us think that God ought to be perfectly capable of doing so too. Whatever the reasons, this is a fairly modern objection to the existence of God, yet a very real and frequent one.

Franz's story, read from the perspective of unbelief, reinforces a particular critique of Christian faith that goes something like this: Christians believe in a God who governs all things. He is a loving God, and therefore wants things to go well in his beloved creation. They hold that everything that happens does so because God wishes it to happen, and because life is generally good, and when things go well, this reinforces their belief that there is a good and loving God. Religious people who believe this, however, are somewhat naive and have not realized the size and presence of evil in the world. When a major tragedy strikes them or the world, it brings into question this simple belief in a good God, making it impossible to believe any longer in his benevolence and kindness.

It is fairly common to find this rather patronizing approach from atheists, who think that believers have never really faced the problem of suffering and that if they did, they would of course give up such naive fantasies as the belief there is a good God. Of course there are some Christian believers who genuinely have never really faced the reality of evil and when it strikes hard, as it did for Ronald Franz, it does shake a hitherto benign and innocent faith.

This kind of sunny faith can only be held by those who have not looked intensely at the cross. As we saw in Chapter 2, the cross can in one sense be seen as the ultimate argument for atheism. It is as if, looking at the cross, we might say, slightly altering Ronald Franz' words: 'I asked God to keep his finger on the shoulder of that one; I told him that boy was special. But he let him die ... I decided I couldn't believe in a God who would let something that terrible happen to a boy like Jesus.'

The existence of suffering does pose a question to a naive faith that has never faced up to the presence of random evil in the world. Yet at the same time, the cross also stands as a major question mark for anyone who gives up faith because they cannot conceive how God can allow evil in his world. Right at the heart of Christian faith stands this most unspeakable fact: that God allowed his Son Jesus to die a cruel and tortured death. And this is not something that lurks at the margins of Christian faith as an odd afterthought: the cross is the universally recognized symbol of Christianity, as recognizable as the Islamic crescent or the Jewish Star of David: it stands on most church steeples, on altars or Communion Tables, and is proudly worn around the necks, or on the lapels of many Christians all around the world.

True Christian faith is not naive about the problem of suffering. Any Christian who has thought deeply about their faith and life in general is very well aware of the horrifying evils that take place in our world, both those inflicted by humans and purely 'natural' evil. And they know that one of those evils stands at the very heart of their faith. It is not that Christians have ignored the uncomfortable fact of evil: they have looked it squarely in the face and still concluded that it is not just possible, but vital to believe in a good and loving God in a world of evil and suffering.

There are many ways in which the Christian faith answers the problem of suffering. There are important philosophical answers that can be given to the question, and this is not the place for those. Our task is to see how suffering looks when viewed through the lens of the cross. How does the scandalous cross of Christ help us find answers to the problem of suffering?

A suffering God?

First of all, the cross tells us that God knows suffering all too well. The insight that the man hanging on the cross is none other than the Son of God, crying out his sense of abandonment by his Father gives us a unique insight into the relationship between God and suffering. God, in the person of the Son, knows what it is to suffer abandonment, agony and death. Whenever the Christian faces suffering of any kind, she knows, even when it does not feel like it, that God stands close by, not as a distant sympathetic observer, but as an intimate participant, as someone who knows intimately what pain is, its nagging, relentless crippling intensity, the tangle of physical, spiritual and emotional pain that is the worst kind.

There is of course, a great deal of joy and laughter in the life and story of Jesus. There are miraculous healings, the elation of Mary and Martha as they see their dead brother Lazarus come back to life, or the tears of the widow from the village of Nain turned to incredulous joy, as she sees her own son sit up alive in the middle of his own funeral procession. There are moments of peace and rest with the disciples, and no doubt times of helpless laughter at his stories of camels going through eyes of needles, or his satirical descriptions of Scribes and Pharisees as like whitewashed gravestones.

111

Yet alongside this there is the pain of misunderstanding, disloyalty, betrayal. He knew the opposition from the very religious leaders who might have welcomed him as God's true Son. He was handed over to his enemies by the treachery of one he had trusted, let down by his closest friend, tried under false charges, sentenced to death illegally, flogged, shamed, nailed to a rough cross and left to die in the hot afternoon sun. 'A man of sorrows and acquainted with grief': that is how the book of Isaiah described the suffering servant, this figure whom he envisaged would one day come to suffer for the sins of the people of Israel, a figure whom Christians quickly associated with Jesus himself, not least because the way his life ended fitted so exactly with Isaiah's description.

Since this is part of the story of Jesus, it is part of the story of God. If Jesus is the unique Son of God, the divine human, then Jesus' suffering is part of God's suffering and so we can say with all seriousness that he is no stranger to our suffering.

At the same time, we also have to say something else about the relationship between God and suffering. We have to say that God rises above

suffering. When the early Christians spoke of
the suffering of Jesus, they were careful to make
a common distinction: that Jesus suffered in his
human, not his divine nature. They also came to
define what was called 'Patripassianism' (the idea
that the Father suffered) as a heresy. To say that
the Father suffered was a step the early Christian
Fathers did not take. Here we are beginning to
delve into some complex Trinitarian Christology
and theology, but it is necessary to understand
the precise way in which the Christian faith faces
suffering.

Why did they want to insist that Jesus suffered
in his human nature? Or that the Father cannot
suffer? Because it was important for them to
say that while God knows what it is to suffer in
Christ, suffering cannot overcome God. There is,
as it were, a part of God that is above and beyond
suffering. If God suffers in all of his being, Father
Son and Holy Spirit, and if God is eternal, then
suffering becomes potentially eternal as well.
Suffering is taken and exalted into the very heart
of God so that it becomes impossible to say
for sure that it will ever come to an end. Now
a central Christian insight into suffering is that
it is real, but temporary. God is eternal, but

suffering and pain are not. In the end, there will be no suffering. As the book of Revelation puts it: 'He will wipe away every tear from their eyes. There will be no more death or mourning or pain, for the old order of things has passed away. (Rev. 21.4)

So when we say that God suffers, we must be careful to check what we are saying. God knows what it is to suffer in the human nature of the incarnate Son, which since the Incarnation has been taken up into God. Yet suffering is simply not strong enough to overcome the eternal God.

The early Fathers tried to express this delicate insight in a number of paradoxes. For example, Cyril of Alexandria used to say that God 'suffers impassibly', trying to catch this sense that God knows suffering intimately in the human nature of the Son, yet he remains beyond and above it, unable to be finally conditioned by it. Martin Luther later wrote of how 'Christ, the impassible Son of God, God and man, was crucified under Pontius Pilate.'[3]

3 Martin Luther, *Disputation on the Divinity and Humanity of Christ*, (1540) Section II.

What this means is that while we can have utter confidence that God knows what it is to suffer in his Son Jesus, at the same time, we can also have utter confidence that suffering is too weak to storm the strongholds of God. Suffering cannot pierce the very essence of God. It does not make it into the new heavens and the new earth. This is the final victory over suffering: God is eternal. And suffering is not.

When we endure some kind of pain, whether physical, emotional or any other kind, there are two things that can make it bearable. One is to know that we are not alone. The other is to know it is temporary. If I suffer a broken leg, or even a broken heart, being with someone who genuinely knows what that pain is like makes all the difference. To know that someone else can empathize (literally to 'suffer with') somehow shares the pain around, as if someone shoulders the burden and weight of pain so that it becomes just a little lighter.

At the same time, knowing that our wounds will one day heal makes all the difference. The unbearable thing is the possibility that it might never end, that suffering and pain have the final word, and that there is absolutely nothing to be done about it.

The Christian insight into suffering tells us that in an ultimate sense, even when we feel alone and in despair over our suffering, that both of these things are true. We are not alone in our suffering, because God, in the person of his Son Jesus, has tasted physical pain, despair, betrayal and death, that he knows intimately what it is to suffer and stands close to us in it. At the same time, suffering is transitory. There is a form of existence that is beyond all suffering: the heart and essence of God, and it is into that heart that we are beckoned in our journey with and into Christ. That is where the journey of faith ends: beyond the possibility of suffering in the heart of God.

The crucified One is risen

That is why, if Jesus really is the divine Son of God, the Resurrection is in fact the obvious thing to have happened to him. If God is ultimately beyond suffering, then death cannot defeat him: God will always win in a battle with death. Life will always triumph.

This is of course the other central proclamation that Christian faith makes in the face of death and suffering: that while suffering is real and strong, God is stronger. Those who stood around the cross on that first Good Friday, watched the best man they had ever known die, and heard the Son of God cry out in his utter loneliness, abandoned by God. Why did they not lose their faith in God? Why did they not become atheists at that point like Ronald Franz? Perhaps they might have done, had they not, three days later, seen him conquer death.

It was not of course that Jesus simply came back to life: there are many instances of people apparently dying and returning back to life – Lazarus is one. In those stories of course, the person concerned still has to die one day. There came another day when Lazarus faced death a second time – for the last time. What happened to Lazarus, the son of the widow of Nain, or the daughter of Jairus, the leader of the Jewish synagogue in Capernaum was resuscitation, not resurrection, and the disciples knew the difference. Jesus was *resurrected*, in other words, rather than returning from the dead, he passed through death and came out the other side, as it were, never to die again.

Here was the ultimate sign that God remains stronger than death, suffering and pain, that they are beaten enemies, that their power is ultimately limited. They can do their worst, but at the end of the day, they fall exhausted before the resilience and irresistible power of the divine life than goes beyond suffering.

In the face of suffering, the Christian faith does not just reassure us that God knows what it is to suffer in the person of Jesus the Son. If that were all to be said, it would be of some comfort, but the message would ultimately still be desolate: that there is no ultimate defence against suffering, no final assurance that it does not have the last word. Knowing someone is with you in your suffering is a help, but ultimately if suffering is the final reality, if everything ends in death and pain, then it is a glimmer of light in the darkness, but darkness wins.

The cross offers more than that. Many Christian churches choose to depict the cross as empty: Jesus no longer hangs upon it, because he is risen, and suffers no more. The empty cross announces that suffering will one day come to an end, that death has been beaten and is a defeated enemy.

What does the cross say to Ronald Franz? Not only does God stand with us in our suffering, he also beats it. He gives us the promise that if we persevere through suffering, we can expect it one day to be behind us. For good.

A soft heart

Christian faith offers us comfort in our suffering. It also offers us ultimate release from our suffering. But in a strange way it also leads us back into it, but in a different form. As Bunyan's pilgrim knew, the path to the high lands of the new heaven and new earth, in which there will be no more weeping or sorrow, passes through some dark valleys, or as St Paul once put it: 'we must go through many hardships to enter the kingdom of God' (Acts 14.22).

Jesus once said to a group of would-be followers, that if they were serious about following him, they would need to 'take up their crosses and follow him'. Anyone in first century Palestine knew what that meant: people who carried crosses were condemned criminals, just as Jesus was soon to be himself. It was a stark and bold image that must have been shocking to those who first heard it: to be a follower of Jesus means to live like a condemned criminal, subject to the taunts and ridicule of others as you wend your way to a certain death.

Now of course for some Christians this meant active persecution for their faith. We are used to stories of the early Christian martyrs, yet it is estimated that more Christians died for the faith in the twentieth century than in all other centuries before it combined, and in the last decade of the twentieth century around 100,000 Christians died for their faith each year.[4] The more intensely and radically we follow Jesus, the more likely persecution and suffering becomes, not less. As Henri de Lubac, the French Roman Catholic theologian put it: 'if the church were more faithful to her mission, she would doubtless often be the more loved, listened to, and more persecuted.'[5]

Yet in many countries today, persecution is a dim and distant shadow. Yes, there are those who will

4 *International Bulletin of Missionary Research*, January 2011.
5 H. de Lubac (1986). *The Splendour of the Church*. San Francisco: Ignatius. p. 200.

publicly attack faith and those who practise it, but the general tolerance of most western societies stops short, at least at present, from active physical persecution of Christians. If this is our situation, does this mean we are excused suffering?

The answer is a fairly clear no. Suffering will inevitably come if anyone tries genuinely to do what is truly good. We may naively think that if we do the right thing, then everything will go well for us. If the pattern of Jesus' life is anything to go by, then this won't work. We will face misunderstanding, opposition and distrust. The great Catholic novelist, Flannery O'Connor writes: 'What people don't realise is how much religion costs. They think faith is a big electric blanket, when of course it is the cross.'

In particular, once you start to try to love people, then it will hurt. In the Old Testament, the cross is prefigured in Israel's experience of exile. Israel is promised a return from exile just as in the New Testament, Christians are promised resurrection after the cross. One of the results of this restoration is that a new heart will be given: 'I will give you a new heart and put a new spirit in you; I will remove from you your heart of stone and

121

give you a heart of flesh' (Ezek. 36.26). A new heart sounds wonderful, until we realize that the problem with soft hearts is that they get damaged more easily and quickly than hard ones. Stony hearts feel less joy, but they also feel less pain. Hard hearts don't get broken. Soft hearts do. There is an easy way to avoid suffering in this life: never love anyone, especially not those worse off than you. The problem is that it may avoid suffering, but it is the road to a shrivelled, dried out, shrunken life – it is the road to hell.

When we understand the cross, not in an intellectual way, but in a deep, personal heartfelt way, when it dawns on us that this was how much the Creator of the Universe loved us, we cannot but find our hearts growing softer. To realize that our deliberate and involuntary sins led Jesus to that lowest point of all, makes us reflect on our own weakness, liability to fail and compromise, and as a result makes us a little less likely to stand in high-handed judgement on others. It softens our hearts towards them. The cross can melt the hardest of heart.

The way to life lies not around the cross but through it, because the way of the cross is the way of love. And love, as we have seen, is in its essence, self-sacrifice. It is the willingness to sacrifice your own comfort, ease and privilege for the sake of someone else. A person who professes love for another, yet who, when the first hint of sacrifice appears on the horizon, takes the road of least resistance and opts for comfort and self-preservation, offers a hollow, empty shell of love. Being the recipient of that kind of professed 'love' is a pretty disillusioning experience. Love goes further – it goes through the cross, through the valley of the shadow of death. Love makes us vulnerable. It is not always thanked, often ignored or misunderstood as manipulative. It gets rejected, abused, does not get the reward it deserves.

And yet, as Christians we can never view the cross other than through the Resurrection. We can never see the cross as the final word about life, humanity, or God. As the end drew near for Jesus, he cried not 'I am finished' but 'It is finished'. It was cry not of resignation and final defeat, but of accomplishment: his suffering was over and the corner had been turned. The enemies of all that is good had done their worst, and they could do no more. Jesus' contemporaries had

123

victory on their minds – victory over the despised Roman occupation. Many, like Judas, thought that the only way to overcome the suffering and exile of the people was by using the Roman method of violence and armed rebellion. Jesus' cry proclaimed victory at the moment of apparent defeat, because it was a victory won not through violence but through love. The only way to overcome violence and suffering was by enduring it, determined to do the right thing, to respond with goodness, patience and forgiveness, until evil has done its worst, in the sure knowledge that evil and suffering are not eternal, and that life will win in the end, as it did three days later.

The Christian answer to suffering is not to avoid it, either intellectually or experientially. It is to point to a picture of suffering at its most intense, the Son of God hanging on a cross out of self-sacrificial love. It is to accept the invitation to 'take up your cross' with Jesus, in the sure and certain knowledge of resurrection, that God ultimately is beyond suffering and so will we be, if we continue our journey with him.

6

THE CROSS AND AMBITION

Do nothing out of selfish ambition or vain conceit. Rather, in humility value others above yourselves, not looking to your own interests but each of you to the interests of the others. In your relationships with one another, have the same attitude of mind Christ Jesus had: Who, being in very nature God, did not consider equality with God something to be used to his own advantage; rather, he made himself nothing by taking the very nature of a servant, being made in human likeness. And being found in appearance as a human being, he humbled himself by becoming obedient to death – even death on a cross! Therefore God exalted him to the highest place and gave him the name that is above every name, that at the name of Jesus every knee should bow, in heaven and on earth and under the earth, and every tongue acknowledge that Jesus Christ is Lord, to the glory of God the Father. (Phil. 2.3–11)

> One of them, an expert in the law, tested
> him with this question: 'Teacher, which
> is the greatest commandment in the
> Law?' Jesus replied: '"Love the Lord your
> God with all your heart and with all your
> soul and with all your mind." This is the
> first and greatest commandment. And the
> second is like it: "Love your neighbour as
> yourself." All the Law and the Prophets
> hang on these two commandments.'
> (Mt. 22.35–40)

Get going. Move forward. Aim High. Plan a takeoff. Don't just sit on the runway and hope someone will come along and push the airplane. It simply won't happen. Change your attitude and gain some altitude. Believe me, you'll love it up here.

These are the words of Donald Trump, the high priest of capitalism, encapsulating the classic wisdom of our age. Implicit within his advice are three assumptions. The first is that the natural trajectory of the person who wants to succeed in life is upwards – Trump speaks down from his lofty vantage point at the pinnacle of the business world beckoning those brave and strong enough to join him in the upper echelons of wealth and power: 'you'll love it up here'. This is the secular version of Ascension.

The second is that in this venture, you are on your own. No-one else will do it for you. You have to launch yourself on the runway of life – the effort is yours, and the credit will be yours. If you wait for someone else to help you, you will be left behind. It is an essentially individualistic view of life, that sees each person as an island of self-reliant independence, a community of one.

The third is that there is an element of competition in all this. If you are on your own and should not expect anyone else to give you a hand, then the route upwards is essentially a solitary one. Not everyone can reach the heights from which Trump speaks, otherwise there would be no-one to look down on. The uphill path to glory is one in which you have to outstrip others on the way leaving the weak behind as you climb towards the stars.

Christian theology has a word for this approach to life. It is called *Pelagianism*. This was the term

used for a set of ideas that emerged in the fourth
century, named after Pelagius, a British ascetic
who lived in Rome, even though it was actually
shaped and radicalized by a number of others
who took his ideas and sharpened them into a
coherent approach to life. Pelagius was a spiritual
advisor to the wealthy Christians of Rome. By
the fourth century, Christianity had become
fashionable, and people flocked to the churches
because it was the thing to do, rather than out of
any great spiritual desire or seriousness. Pelagius'
answer to this rather nominal, lax Christianity
was to urge those who came to him for spiritual
advice to do just what Donald Trump suggests:
pull up their socks, work harder and they will
ascend the spiritual ladder, just as we hope today
to climb the economic or social ladder.

Pelagianism told people that there is a God who
beckons us upwards, and this God has given us all
we need to succeed. He has given us instructions
(the law), the capacity to obey those instructions
(free will) and a model to follow (the example of
Jesus). But then, crucially, God leaves us to it,
waiting to see if we will avail ourselves of these
aids and start climbing. Again, essentially, we are
on our own, and whether or not we reach the

heights of the spiritual life depends on us and the
effort we put into it.

Pelagius originally came to the notice of the wider
Church when he took exception to a prayer of
St Augustine which seemed to him to imply that
we were helpless to do anything on our own, and
instead needed to wait languidly and passively
for God to come and help us – to give a push to
the aeroplane of our life waiting on the tarmac.
It all seemed to Pelagius to lack a proper sense of
ambition and drive. A debate followed, between
Augustine and Pelagius and his followers which
reached something of a conclusion in 418, at the
Council of Carthage, in which Pelagianism was
finally judged to be a Christian heresy – an idea
that is almost right, but if taken further would
end up unravelling Christian faith altogether.

Christian ambition

Augustine's response was not to dent the need
for proper ambition, but to re-direct it. He
argued that Pelagianism was just too simple. It
did not do justice to the complexity of human
psychology and motivation. We are not as free as
we would like to think. Our hearts are shaped by
all kinds of forces outside our control, and most

importantly, our hearts and minds are damaged in that they are unable to see the true value of things. In particular, God, the most beautiful and wonderful being imaginable, actually seems dull and uninteresting to us.

We are incapable of grasping his beauty, just as if we were a children in an art gallery wondering what all the fuss was about Botticelli's Venus or Michelangelo's David, or someone who just doesn't get football watching a piece of sporting genius and being unable to appreciate its value. Unless God gives us the desire to love him above all else we simply do not find him at all desirable. We will just be pulled one way and another by our unruly desires and never focus upon what is truly good and beautiful – God himself.

Augustine's solution was not however, what Pelagius thought it was – a passive, indolent lack of ambition. Augustine had a proper sense of ambition and ascension. He too said that we must 'press forward to that perfect and full righteousness in which there shall be perfect and full love in the sight of his glory.'[1] The human destiny

1 *On Man's Perfection in Righteousness VIII, 18*, Augustine

is to ascend to fellowship with God, but it starts with pointing the pilgrim in exactly the opposite direction from that which Pelagius advised.

Pelagius instructed his spiritual clients to start working hard, setting out on their own towards the gates of heaven. Augustine says that the first step is not one we make at all, but one that God makes, by his grace, kindling within us the first faint hints of a love for God. The kind of ambition Augustine offers is a fierce ambition to be perfected in love: 'Let us run, believing, hoping, longing; let us run, subjugating the body, cheerfully and heartily doing alms – in giving kindnesses and forgiving injuries, praying that our strength may be helped as we run; and let us so listen to the commandments which urge us to perfection, as not to neglect running towards the fullness of love.'[2]

The key for Augustine is love. Our ambition should consist of the desire to be full to the brim of love. Yet the ability to love is not under

(1991). *Anti-Pelagian Writings*. Edinburgh: T & T Clark. p. 164.
2 Ibid. *VIII, 19,* p. 165.

our control. We cannot simply choose to love someone or something – love is always caught up with desire and we cannot always control our desires. So the path to salvation begins with God stirring in our hearts a sense of how good and desirable God is, so that we begin to love him above everything else. In turn then, we start to love our neighbours, in accord with Jesus' teaching: 'Love the Lord your God with all your heart and with all your soul and with all your strength and with all your mind'; and, 'Love your neighbour as yourself.'

The one goal of Christian life is to become like God, the God whose essential characteristic is love. That is real ambition. In fact it is the only ambition really worth having. Whatever else you aim at in life, do not miss out on the one thing that is the most valuable of them all: to become capable of disinterested, selfless love. There are few people who can really do this. Most of us find it very hard to really seek the good of others beyond ourselves. Schooled by years of bad experience, where unless we look ourselves no-one else will, we settle for the regular, ordinary way of living, of each to his own, looking after number one. We become hardened in these habits, becoming simply incapable of doing anything else beyond the most trivial acts of self-sacrifice.

Christian faith is not devoid of ambition. The German philosopher, Friedrich Nietzsche despised the cross as the central symbol of Christianity because it spoke to him of passivity and a lack of drive. He described it as 'the seductive, intoxicating, anaesthetizing, and corrupting power of that symbol of the "holy cross", that horrific paradox of the "crucified God", that mystery of an inconceivably ultimate, most extreme cruelty and self-crucifixion.'[3] For him, the cross was the sign of a deadening, life-denying religion devoid of all energy and vitality. Yet he missed the point. The cross does point us towards an ambition: the ambition to become capable of that kind of self-sacrificial love, the kind of love that enhances life and relationships.

So the difference between Donald Trump and Pelagius on the one hand, and Jesus and Augustine on the other is not that the former are ambitious and the latter are not. Both are equally ambitious;

3 F. Nietzsche (1996). *On The Genealogy of Morals*. Oxford: Oxford University Press. p. 21.

both urge their followers to strive for the best. It is just that their understanding of what is the best is radically different. Trump and his kind are fixed on striving for trivial things like money, cars, political or economic power. Jesus and Augustine set their sights far higher: on being someone perfected in love.

Ambition reborn

So how do we set out on that road? If Donald Trump and Pelagius urge us to be self-starters, climbing the first rung of the ladder towards success, the alternative wisdom of Christian faith tells us to start climbing downwards, not upwards.

When St Paul writes to the Christians in Philippi about how they are to conduct themselves, he lays out the same path as that of Jesus before him and Augustine after him. Paul too writes of 'striving side by side for the faith of the gospel' (1.27) and 'work(ing) out your own salvation in fear and trembling' (2.12), yet when he expands what this actually means, he turns to the cross as the pattern of life of the Christian.

Christ Jesus was in the form of God, equal with God the Father. In other words, rather than starting from the bottom, Christ begins in the highest place. He then descends, 'taking the very nature of a servant ... humbled himself, by becoming obedient to death – even death on a cross' (2.7f.). The pattern is not the Trumpian ascent to glory, but first it is the descent to the depths. And precisely because Jesus took this path, he is then the one who has 'exalted him to the highest place ... that at the name of Jesus every knee should bow, in heaven and on earth and under the earth, and every tongue acknowledge that Jesus Christ is Lord' (vv. 9–11).

When we consider Jesus on the first Good Friday, one of the most remarkable things is the focus of his attention. On his way to the cross he looks at the women who are wailing their grief and says: 'Daughters of Jerusalem, do not weep for me; weep for yourselves and for your children. For the time will come when you will say, "Blessed are the childless women, the wombs that never bore and the breasts that never nursed!"'

He turns to the thief and says to him 'today you will be with me in paradise'. He looks at the crowds gathered around the base of the cross, brought together by a ghoulish fascination with watching the slow suffering and death of the poor unfortunate victims, and he says 'Forgive them Father for they know not what they do.'

He turns to the few who have faithfully stayed with him through his ordeal, and tells his disciple John to take care of his mother: 'Woman here is your son – here is your mother.' The whole time, remarkably, his attention is not on himself and his own suffering, it is on those around him, both his friends and his enemies. This is what it means, to be the ultimate servant of others. This is the pattern of Christian life.

This is what ambition looks like when viewed through the cross. If the cross is taken seriously as the starting point for our thinking about God and the life we are to live, then ambition is not negated, but radically re-directed.

First, the direction of travel is reversed. There is ascent here, but the pathway here is first descent before ascent, the path downward before the path upward. And this simply means the path of love. This pattern, replicated in the life of an ordinary human being means this: 'in humility value others above yourselves, not looking to your own interests but each of you to the interests of the others' (2.4).

This is in fact as good a definition of love as you can find – it is the ability to be a servant of others, to see others shine rather than yourself, to be more interested to hear others' stories than to tell your own, to be more pleased at others' successes than your own, to be focused not first and foremost on what serves your purposes and wellbeing, but what serves the purpose and wellbeing of others.

When we see this quality in others, it is deeply attractive. Occasionally you meet someone like this, who is genuinely interested in you, who wants to know all about you, not because they are inquisitive but because you seem to matter to them. It is a rare thing, but when you do meet someone like that, it somehow satisfies something deep within. We are not always so sure we want to be that way ourselves, but in others, at least, it is wonderful to experience. The way up starts with the way down.

Second, the goal of ambition is transformed. Those who live in the light of the cross are deeply ambitious. They work hard and aim for the best, but that 'best' is to be someone capable of perfect, pure love for God and for others. That may involve riches and fame, but it may not – in fact whether it does or not is immaterial, except insofar as any wealth that comes our way is to be used as a tool for loving other people, pursuing their best interests instead of our own, making just a small dent in the scandal of inequality that leaves vast numbers of people in poverty in a world where there is enough to go round.

This is not self-flagellation, a self-hatred that masks deep insecurity. 'Preferring others before ourselves' is not pretending others are better than us at some particular skill, when we know right well that we are more capable or skilled than they are. The person who has learnt the way of the cross is not thinking of their own humility. They are not in fact thinking of themselves at all, but instead their thoughts are occupied by the needs of their neighbour: how can I bless or enrich someone else today?

True humility comes not from a sense of worthlessness, but the opposite, a sense of our own

true worth, loved by God not for our achievements, or our successes but simply because we are
his beloved children. This sense of being loved
breeds a deep security that cannot be shaken by
failure or disaster, because it is rooted not in our
fortunes but in God's faithfulness.

Third, the nature of our relationships is changed.
Looking through the cross, it becomes possible
to conceive of a better way to relate to others
than the competitive urge that wants to see
others fail because it makes us feel better about
ourselves. Georg Maior, the sixteenth century
reformer put this in a typically earthy medieval
way, commenting on this text from Philippians:
'Since the divine majesty humbled himself so
deeply on account of me that he became my
servant, servant of all of us, how is that we
pathetic excrement and maggot-sacks are so
proud and arrogant? We despise each other, and
each one of us yearns to be greater and better
than the other. Tell me, what am I and what are
you? Are we not dust and ashes taken from the
earth that will return again to the earth, as we see
daily before our eyes? How much more should I
on account of this humble myself and serve my

neighbour, since I observe such humility and love in the high and divine majesty!'[4]

The Trumpian ambition, to rise beyond the also-rans to become famous, wealthy and admired, is, as we have seen, an essentially solitary vision. Pelagius, likewise, had an essentially individualistic view of the human race. We are all on our own, independent, free to choose, climbing the strenuous path to salvation. Augustine on the other hand had a more corporate view – we are not free, autonomous individuals, but are each part of the human race, bound to each other in subtle ways we barely recognize. The path laid out by the cross, where each person looks out for the interests of others is in fact ultimately a vision of community, not of individual achievement: this is the way human society was meant to work.

The road to happiness

It is also the way to true happiness. The American theologian Ellen Charry writes: 'the classic theologians based their understanding of human excellence on knowing and loving

4 Georg Maior, *Auslegung der Epistel S. Pauli an die Philipper*, 122r–v.

God, the imitation of and assimilation to whom brings proper human dignity and flourishing … (they) held that knowing and loving God is the mechanism of choice for forming excellent character and promoting genuine happiness.'[5]

To become like God, to learn to love, seems to us like the way to loss, becoming vulnerable and empty. In fact, says Christian wisdom, the exact opposite is true. To learn to love like this is in fact to begin to build a life that is satisfied and healthy, because it is the only way of life that connects us with each other.

The kind of ambition that Donald Trump recommends is essentially a lonely way of life: me against the world. I might get to the top of the pile, but when I am there, when I achieve my ambition, I find myself in solitary isolation, not sure whether I can trust anyone else. I have beaten all my rivals but the cost is loneliness. The alternative, Christian ambition, to become a person capable of love, is a communal vision of life. Only love binds

5   E. Charry (1997). *By the Renewing of Your Minds: The Pastoral Function of Christian Doctrine.* New York: Oxford University Press. p. 18.

us to one another, only people who have learnt to love can create relationship and community. One of the most painful and devastating sicknesses of our time is loneliness, and a way of life that builds community and can enable friendship is infinitely to be preferred to one that breeds isolation, however many cars, houses and fancy holidays it offers.

Imagine for a moment a culture where everyone's main aim was to seek the good of their neighbour, where the only social competitiveness was to find ways to bless the person next door. This would be a community where you no longer had to worry about your own fortunes or future – that is taken care of by others. Your only concern was to ensure that your neighbour was looked after, that her needs were taken care of, that she had what she needed to survive and thrive. That would be a community where there was genuine mutuality, real co-operation – it would be real community, rather than the shadow version of the real thing that we so commonly experience today.

The biblical scholar Richard Bauckham writes of how the ancient world was divided into masters and slaves. In the modern world, we are all our own masters. In the Kingdom of God, we all learn to be slaves of one another.[6] This is the new world brought about by the cross, the new way opened up to us when we look at the world through the lens of Calvary. It may seem impossible, yet this is the way human society was meant to work, oriented around the ambition of love not self-centred aspiration.

And the reason why this is the way the world was meant to work is that this is the nature of God. If, as we have seen, the cross not just the means of salvation, but is also a revelation of God, it tells us that this is the very nature of God to love the world so much as to give himself, in the form of his only Son, so that it might be rescued and reversed in direction, turned back towards God rather than hurtling away from him. It is in the nature of God to seek the good of others before his own. Or to put it as simply as the New Testament does, God is Love.

That means that when we do the most ordinary things for the sake of another, when a parent

6 R. Bauckham (2002). *God and the Crisis of Freedom: Biblical and Contemporary Perspectives*, Louisville: Westminster John Knox, p. 15.

waits for their teenage child outside a party
late at night, when a young woman washes an
elderly relative, when the Chair stacks the chairs
after a meeting, when a host washes up so that
others can enjoy the rest of the evening, when
an educated graduate chooses to live in a rough
area of a city so that he can be a good neighbour
to the homeless, refugees and immigrants who
live all around – when we do these things, that is
when we are at our most God-like. It is when we
love, when we choose to be the servants of others
rather than their masters.

Of course this is hugely counter-intuitive. We
naturally think to be like God is to be in charge,
to be grand, important, looked up to by everyone.
This is why the powerful usually misunderstand
God – they assume that God is like them. As Martin
Luther once put it: 'To no one does the preaching
of the cross appear so foolish as to philosophers and men of power because it is completely
contrary to them and to their sensitivities.'[7]

The cross shows us a different God – a humble
God who is willing to take the form of a servant

7   WA 56.174.4–10.

for the sake of his creation. It is the last thing we would expect from our normal expectation of God-like behaviour, but as we learn at the outset of this journey, we need to learn to revise our understandings of God, our expectations of what he should be like, in the light of the cross.

This is why we may have more to learn from cleaners, gardeners and dinner ladies than we do from CEOs, oligarchs and government ministers (although the latter should give us a clue – the fact that we often call our political leaders 'ministers' is a remnant of this Christian understanding of leadership, as 'minister' is none other than the Latin word for 'servant').

The Church is intended to be the community where this becomes visible. It is hard to imagine the whole of western civilization changed into this vision of communal life, each looking after their neighbour's interests before their own. These words were first addressed to this tiny community of Christians in Philippi, a group of perhaps fifty people. There is wisdom in starting small. If it can happen in a small community like a local church, or even a family, then that can become a sign of the new world that the cross points to.

Small local communities of Christians are potentially the seedbed of a new world, places where people learn to lay aside the usual ambitions, to create the beginnings of a community of people looking out for each other, where in humility, each one values others above themselves, not looking to their own interests but to the interests of the others. If that vision were to be taken seriously in every church, however small, and begin to spread into the local communities surrounding those churches, then a vision of that new world might gradually come into sight, as each one becomes a hint, a foretaste to signpost to the future that will one day be.

7

The Cross and Failure

While Peter was below in the courtyard,
one of the servant girls of the high priest
came by. When she saw Peter warming
himself, she looked closely at him. "You
also were with that Nazarene, Jesus," she
said. But he denied it. "I don't know or
understand what you're talking about,"
he said, and went out into the entryway.
When the servant girl saw him there,
she said again to those standing around,
"This fellow is one of them." Again
he denied it. After a little while, those
standing near said to Peter, "Surely you
are one of them, for you are a Galilean."
He began to call down curses, and he
swore to them, "I don't know this man
you're talking about." Immediately the
rooster crowed the second time. Then
Peter remembered the word Jesus had
spoken to him: "Before the rooster
crows twice you will disown me three
times." And he broke down and wept.
(Mk 14.66–72)

The other problem with ambition is when it goes wrong. We all have ambitions of one kind or another when we set our sights on a goal – promotion at work, a new relationship, performing in front of others, winning a game. And when we achieve those ambitions it is intensely satisfying, the more so if it was truly ambitious, a goal that in the first place we doubted we could achieve. Yet when we fail, it leaves us empty. TV talent shows, or annual award ceremonies focus on the winners, not the losers. The losers disappear into the background, licking their wounds and nursing their hurts. What does the cross then say to them? What does failure look like, viewed from the cross?

The entry of Jesus into Jerusalem had caused something of a stir. Jesus had chosen not to walk into the city, as he usually did, but to ride in, with his supporters laying down palms in front of him in a demonstration designed to proclaim the arrival of a king. This was a deliberately provocative allusion to the prophecy of Zechariah, which referred to the coming of the Son of David – the king promised ever since the days of the great King David, the highest and best of the Old Testament Israelite monarchs. And that is exactly what the crowds thought they were seeing: 'Blessed is he who comes in the name of the Lord! Blessed is the coming kingdom of our father David!'

Returning the next day, climbing up an impressive wide stairway, across the bridge into the Temple itself, Jesus proceeded to stage an acted drama, a public act of rebellion, predicting the destruction of this magnificent Herodian edifice, the pride of Jerusalem itself. Striding into the area where officials exchanged the various monies of the Jewish diaspora into Tyrian shekels, the common currency which enabled pilgrims to buy items for sacrifice, Jesus marched through, gripping the tables and hurling them into the air, scattering the coins everywhere, shouting his slogan 'Is it not written: "My house will be called a house of prayer for all nations"? But you have made it a den of robbers!'

It was a relatively small affair, violent, noisy but brief, over as soon as it started. Jesus succeeded in temporarily stopping all business in the temple, bringing it to a standstill for a short while, but managed to escape before an inevitable cohort of Roman soldiers was dispatched to arrest yet

149

another troublemaker in what must have seemed just the latest bout of unrest in the Temple.

If he managed to escape arrest that day, it was not to last. Before long he was in custody, hauled before the Sanhedrin to answer charges of sedition. What might have appeared as an attempt to overthrow the powers that be in Jerusalem, a prediction of divine judgement on the Temple and its rulers had, it seemed, ended in failure.

Meanwhile, while Jesus is being tried before the Sanhedrin, Peter, his headstrong follower and unpredictable friend tries his best to stay as close as he dare. Caught between fidelity, a sense of duty towards his mentor and fear for his own skin, he had been with Jesus throughout, following on behind as he rode down the Mount of Olives, scattered the moneychangers, rampaged through the Temple and finally met his arrest in the garden. Now, Peter loiters unconvincingly in the courtyard just below the lighted room where Jesus awaits his fate, eventually falling asleep in a dark corner of the yard.

As the dawn breaks, and as the city stirs, he warms himself by an early morning fire. One of the High

Priest's kitchen maids, aware of the prisoner who had undergone intensive questioning upstairs overnight, spots him and begins to accuse him of being an ally of Jesus. He tries to brush off the suggestion. She gathers a few others who are equally sure he is implicated somehow in the rebellion. Forced to choose between loyalty and safety, he instinctively plumps for the latter, more and more emphatically denying he knows anything about Jesus, turning the air blue with his curses.

As his denials get stronger, his evasion blacker, the cock crows.

The anatomy of failure

Most people we meet seem pretty together. Walk through any city street and most people look in control, self-possessed, going about their business in a measured and contented way. Under the surface however, shadows lurk. Under the veneer of competence, pockets of self-doubt lie within most of us, fuelled by either the memory or fear of failure. It may be a parent who was never satisfied, always wanting more, a friend, lover or spouse who walked out, and deep down you suspect it was because of some inadequacy in yourself,

151

some flaw of character that made the break-up inevitable. Or it may be the feeling that someday, someone will find you out. If your friends only knew what you were like, if your boss knew how little you really know, if your darkest secrets of inadequacy or incompetence were made visible, then surely disgrace would follow fast.

The irony is that we all think we are the only one. Everyone else seems untouched by failure, immune to the dead weight it inflicts on the soul. The memory or fear of failure is usually something we carry alone until it is forced out of us into the open.

Peter's story of following Jesus had been a litany of failure. Even before this, at several crucial moments he had fallen short. He had boldly tried to copy Jesus' feat of walking on water, but after a few initial successful steps, he had sunk faster than a stone. During a trip away with Jesus and James and John two of his other closest friends, Peter, caught up in his enthusiasm, completely missed the point when Jesus was suddenly and dazzlingly transfigured. Now, as the morning cock crows, this is the moment of his deepest failure yet. There are moments in life when we feel on trial, where our very core is being examined. And this is one of them. Just as Jesus was on trial in the room above, Peter was on trial in the courtyard below.

He had only recently pledged his undying loyalty to Jesus. Only the night before, he had promised, on his life, swearing blind that whatever the other cowards will do, he would NEVER walk away. Jesus could absolutely depend on him. And now as the cock crowed, just as Jesus had said, the pattern of failure had repeated itself. Peter had failed in the most devastating way possible. This was not just misplaced enthusiasm or misunderstanding; it was deliberate, emphatic, blasphemous failure.

Peter's story is classic tragedy: it is Ovid's Icarus, Shakespeare's King Lear, Milton's Lucifer. The higher we set our sights, the further it is to fall. Failure is more traumatic when we aim too high. And yet to aim too low is to risk blandness and mediocrity. If Peter had stayed as an ordinary Jewish Galilean fisherman, he would not have felt this sense of crushing failure. If he had not claimed so categorically his own determination to remain true, he wouldn't have felt so wretched.

This is the nature of failure – we can avoid it if we never try anything, but ambition is a risky thing when it goes wrong.

Public shame

There are two quite remarkable things about this story. The first is that it was told at all. Why did Mark include it in his gospel (and subsequently, Matthew, Luke and John as well – it is one of the few stories that make it into all four gospels)? By the time the gospels were written down, Peter had been a well-known and established figure in the early Church, and if tradition is right, the first overseer of the Church in the city of Rome, the centre of the empire. He was a celebrity, perhaps the best known Christian of them all, someone before whom even Paul at times felt a little cowed. When you think about it, is surprising that this story was not hushed up, kept quiet and suppressed, after all, it hardly reflects well on this leading figure in the emerging Christian movement.

The general consensus amongst most New Testament scholars is that Mark was the first gospel to be written. If so, then this is where it was first written down and enshrined within authorized early Christian literature. The other gospels presumably copied it in adapted form from Mark. So back to the question – why did Mark include it in his gospel?

There is a fairly strong early tradition about how Mark's gospel came to be written. Papias was an early Christian writer of the second century. At one stage he records the link between Mark and Peter:

> Mark, who had been Peter's interpreter,
> wrote down carefully, but not in order, all
> that he remembered of the Lord's sayings
> and doings. For he had not heard the
> Lord or been one of his followers, but
> later, as I said, one of Peter's. Peter used
> to adapt his teaching to the occasion,
> without making a systematic arrangement
> of the Lord's sayings, so that Mark was
> quite justified in writing down some
> things just as he recalled them. For
> he had one purpose only: to leave out
> nothing that he had heard, and to make
> no misstatement of it.[1]

1 Eusebius (1965). *The History of the Church*. London: Penguin. p. 152.

If Papias is right (and there is no particular reason to doubt him), Mark's primary source for his gospel was Peter. Many hours of listening to Peter's stories about Jesus had enabled him to write down fairly accurately what Peter had regularly taught. If the story of Peter's failure made it into Mark's account, there is only one realistic explanation for how it got there: Peter himself used to tell the story again and again. This shameful, embarrassing story, the lowest moment of Peter's life was repeatedly re-told, not by Peter's enemies to discredit him, but by Peter himself.

Today, if a celebrity has any shameful secret in their past, a mistress, tax avoidance, a sleazy drunken night that ended up in a cell, the normal practice is to try to cover it up, and make sure it stays out of the tabloids. Peter's approach is startlingly different. He seems to have told the story over and over, emphasizing and re-visiting the moment of his own shame and failure. There is a well-known bit of pollster's advice for anyone wanting to get elected: 'enhance your positives; minimize your negatives'. This seems to go against this entirely. This is Peter minimizing his positives and enhancing his negatives!

The second surprising thing is that this was not the end of the road for Peter. After this catastrophic failure, the natural thing would have been to retire to Galilee, to 'spend more time with his family' as the normal excuse goes. Political careers don't usually survive massive public embarrassment. The damage is too great and rehabilitation too risky. Yet not long after this we see Peter, right in the middle of the group as the leader, or spokesman of the followers of Jesus, deciding who will replace Judas (Acts 1.15ff.) and standing in public in the heart of Jerusalem, explaining to the bemused crowds the strange phenomenon of the day of Pentecost (Acts 2.14ff.). It is as if nothing had happened. Somehow, within a few weeks of this moment of disaster, he had been restored.

Failure does not destroy Peter. In fact it re-creates him. In one sense it is as if nothing has changed, but in another, something significant had shifted in him. The boldness and courage that led him to speak to the crowds on the day of Pentecost was not quite there beforehand. The Peter of the book of Acts speaks with a command and authority which the earlier version just didn't have. There is an episode when Peter is confronted by a beggar as he is entering the Temple. The authority with which Peter speaks is unmistakable:

> Peter looked straight at him, as did John.
> Then Peter said: "Look at us!" So the
> man gave them his attention, expecting
> to get something from them. Then Peter
> said: "Silver and gold I do not have, but
> what I do have I give you. In the name
> of Jesus of Nazareth, walk." Taking him
> by the right hand, he helped him up
> and instantly the man's feet and ankles
> became strong. (Acts 3.4–7)

This is a different person altogether from the cocky yet fragile figure we meet in the gospels. Later in his life, or so the story goes, he was presented again with the choice of whether to deny or stay loyal to Jesus. This time, he did what he should have done first time round. Eusebius, the greatest of the early Christian historians records that during Nero's persecution in the early 60s AD, Peter was arrested, charged with being a Christian, and then crucified upside down, in a grotesque imitation of the very Lord he had denied thirty years before.

Failure our teacher

Who learns something in this episode of Peter's failure? Is it Jesus? Does he learn something new about Peter that he didn't know before? That Peter, who seemed so solid and 'rock-like' was in fact weak and not to be trusted? The exchange which took place back when Peter claimed absolute loyalty to Jesus suggests otherwise. When Peter brashly promises that he will never be unfaithful, Jesus knows the weakness that lies behind the bravado, which is why he predicts, accurately as it turns out, that Peter will fail at the first hurdle, before twenty-four hours have passed. Jesus learns nothing new about Peter here that he didn't know before.

The one who learns something is Peter. Jesus' view of Peter does not change, but Peter's view of Peter does. He realizes something about himself that he did not really know before – that he is not the person he thought he was. The claim that he was somehow superior to the others who might abandon Jesus in his hour of need, the boast that he would be able to stand when others fell away was, in reality, hollow and empty. Failure had opened Peter's eyes to himself in a way that success never could. It had led him to a level of self-knowledge that went beyond anything he knew before. He went away from the courtyard a despairing, but a wiser man.

The same has been true for many people. Success tends to confirm our rosiest pictures of who we are. Success substantiates our fond belief that really we are exceptional, or at least not in need of any great improvement. Failure on the other hand teaches uncomfortable lessons. It can help us to see we are not the people we thought we were, that underneath the surface lie all kinds of hidden and not-so-hidden desires that are not as innocent as we might like to think.

In 2008, J. K. Rowling, the famous author of the Harry Potter books was invited to give the commencement address at Harvard University. Faced with the bright young graduates of the Ivy League, she chose to speak on 'The Fringe Benefits of Failure and the Importance of the Imagination.' Reflecting on a period of her life when she was a jobless single parent after a brief disastrous marriage, with no income and few prospects, she wrote:

So why do I talk about the benefits of
failure? Simply because failure meant
a stripping away of the inessential. I
stopped pretending to myself that I was
anything other than what I was … Failure
gave me an inner security that I had
never attained by passing examinations.
Failure taught me things about myself
that I could have learned no other way.

Failure can open our eyes to ourselves in a way
that success seldom can. It can lead to a proper
honesty and realism about who we are and of
what we are capable. In a sense, failure is a part
of growing up.

Yet of course, failure does not always lead in this
direction. Peter was not the only person who
failed in the sorry tale of Jesus' arrest, trial and
crucifixion. Judas was also one of the inner circle,
one of the chosen ones, who faced a similar
choice. His was different – not so much a choice
between loyalty and safety, but between different
visions of the future. Was it a love of money? Was
it disillusionment over Jesus' failure to deliver
political independence for Israel? For whatever
reason – the gospels do not give us a clear answer

as to why he chose to do what he did – Judas gave up on Jesus and decided to hand him over to the Jewish authorities. Judas, like Peter, is confronted at a later stage with his betrayal of Jesus, and Matthew tells us that Judas was later filled with remorse at what he had done, just like Peter.

Yet Peter's story and Judas' end in very different places. Judas' remorse ends in despair and ultimate suicide. Peter's ends in restoration and transformation. Why the difference? Presumably Peter could also have allowed his failure to lead him into the despondency of having failed the one big test of his life. He could have made excuses and returned quietly to his former life. The fact that he was not only restored, but that he made sure that the story of his failure was re-told repeatedly in the early Church, whenever the story of Jesus' Passion was recounted, tells us that he took the hard but vital decision to look failure in the face, accept what it told him about himself and allow it to rebuild him.

How was Peter able to do that? The key is found in a small episode recounted in John's gospel. After Jesus' crucifixion and resurrection, he meets with his disciples back in Galilee where it all started.

In the meantime Peter had done exactly what we might expect him to do – he had returned home, tail between his legs, presumably resolved never to pin his hopes on a messiah again. Picking up his previous job, he was out on the lake, brooding, fishing, trying to rebuild his life into some kind of normality, even though frustratingly even that was not going well, with the fish lying near the bottom, stubbornly refusing to be caught.

And there, suddenly, is Jesus. There follows a conversation painful in its intensity and honesty. Jesus asks Peter the question that he had failed so spectacularly to answer back in Jerusalem: 'Do you love me?' All of Peter's actions on that fateful night had led to one conclusion: no, Peter did not really love Jesus. If he had, he wouldn't have denied him. And yet Jesus keeps asking him, drawing out from him the response, 'Yes – despite what I did, I do love you – you know I do.'

Peter's view of himself had changed radically. There is perhaps an honesty, a depth of meaning in these professions of love that was not there before. Yet he realizes that Jesus' view of him has not changed one iota. There is no rebuke, no recriminations, no blame. Only acceptance, forgiveness, love. Jesus' view of him was not dependent on his success as a disciple and it was unaffected by his failure. And it was perhaps this simple lesson that was the secret of Peter's ability to rebuild – to stop the spiral into despair and self-destruction that had overtaken Judas, and enabled him to start again.

Overcoming failure

When we fail, one of our biggest fears is what others will think. Can we really lift our head up in public again, knowing that everyone knows our shame? Looking through the cross, we see a different meaning to failure. When we fail, God learns nothing new about us. He is not disappointed by our fall, as if it was unexpected. Just as it was for Peter, his feeling towards us, his regard for us is exactly the same as before. Failure need not destroy us, but only if we look both it and God directly in the face. Failure can lead to self-knowledge and wisdom if we refuse to make the excuses that will readily come to mind, and let it tell us what we need to hear about ourselves: that we are frail, liable to miss the mark, perhaps most often we are at our most confident. We are sinners in need of forgiveness.

Failure is not just about self-knowledge though – it is also about divine knowledge. It can lead to restoration if we allow it to turn us back to, rather than away from God. Looking steadfastly into the face of God, which is none other than the face of Jesus Christ, as Peter was forced to do on that cold morning by the lakeside, is the only way to be recalled to the steady, patient and constant heart of God – a heart that knows exactly what we are like, but reaches out in love and forgiveness anyway.

John Calvin began his famous 'Institutes' with the words: 'Nearly all the wisdom we possess, that is to say, true and sound wisdom, consists of two parts: the knowledge of God and of ourselves.'[2] Whatever else we know, this is true wisdom: to know who we are, and to know who God is. There are few things better than failure to teach us both.

This is a message for lousy Christians. If you think you have failed as a Christian, that all the others are better than you, they pray longer, drink less, feel less lustful, evangelize more effectively,

2   Calvin, *Institutes* Ii.1.

then this is a story for you. Jesus died for you, not because you are a good Christian, but because you are a bad one. God loves lousy Christians, failed Christians, honest Christians. In fact he is likely most often to use those who know they are lousy Christians. It is no accident that Peter the failure became the central figure in early Christianity. Jesus predicted that he would build his church on the 'rock' that was Peter (Mt. 16.18) in full awareness that he would fail badly, and this word came true as well. The story of the cross introduces us to a God who loves failures: in fact he can do more with failures than he can with those who have never experienced their own frailty and weakness.

Of course he does not want us to continue to fail. He wants instead to rebuild us so that we are less likely to in future, less fragile, more robust, reliable and likely to stick to our word both towards ourselves, others and towards God. Yet the path to faithfulness usually begins with a recognition of unfaithfulness. The path to the Father's house usually begins in the pigsty.

Those who, like Peter, set out falteringly to follow Jesus are not guaranteed immunity from failure or even the odd moment of despair. On the contrary, we are promised the possibility of using failure as a road to both self-knowledge and knowledge of God. It can teach us both how far we are capable of falling, but that also our true value lies not in our achievements or successes but in the fact that we are addressed by a God who looks us in the eye, as he did with Peter, and says, regardless of our failure, 'Follow me'.

8
THE CROSS AND
RECONCILIATION

For God was pleased to have all his
fullness dwell in him, and through him
to reconcile to himself all things, whether
things on earth or things in heaven, by
making peace through his blood, shed on
the cross. Once you were alienated from
God and were enemies in your minds
because of your evil behaviour. But now
he has reconciled you by Christ's physical
body through death to present you
holy in his sight, without blemish and
free from accusation— if you continue
in your faith, established and firm, and
do not move from the hope held out in
the gospel. This is the gospel that you
heard and that has been proclaimed to
every creature under heaven, and of
which I, Paul, have become a servant.
(Col. 1.19–22)

Therefore, remember that formerly you who are Gentiles by birth and called "uncircumcised" by those who call themselves "the circumcision" (which is done in the body by human hands) – remember that at that time you were separate from Christ, excluded from citizenship in Israel and foreigners to the covenants of the promise, without hope and without God in the world. But now in Christ Jesus you who once were far away have been brought near by the blood of Christ. For he himself is our peace, who has made the two one and has destroyed the barrier, the dividing wall of hostility, by setting aside in his flesh the law with its commands and regulations. His purpose was to create in himself one new humanity out of the two, thus making peace, and in one body to reconcile both of them to God through the cross, by which he put to death their hostility. He came and preached peace to you who were far away and peace to those who were near. For through him we both have access to the Father by one Spirit. (Eph. 2.11–18)

As the early Christians thought through the implications of the death of Christ on the cross for their own world, it began to dawn on them that this event did not just win personal salvation, but promised a new social order.

These Christians saw the cross as the means by which God had reconciled all things to himself. Through this event, harmony had returned to a broken and disjointed world. A world that was in revolt against God had been reconciled to him. As we saw in Chapter 2, the cross has healed the wound at the heart of the creation, and brought harmony where before there was discord. Yet this harmony has definite social and even political consequences: it led to a different vision of human society, a different way of relating than could be found anywhere else in the first century world.

This first century Mediterranean world was deeply divided. Just as the eastern bloc once held together a collection of different nations and people under the banner of Communism, the Roman Empire also imposed an uneasy truce over a collection of different ethnic and tribal identities. Take a city such as Antioch for example. This was a settlement originally formed by two groups, Syrians and Greeks, with each community living in a different section of the town, separated from the other by walls. As the city grew, Jews arrived from Palestine, along with slaves from various parts of the empire. When the city became part of the Roman Empire in 64 BC, many Romans started to arrive, along with Gauls, Germans and members of other 'barbarian' tribes. Historians and archaeologists suggest that Antioch during the first century was divided into eighteen different areas, for eighteen different ethnic groups. These factions lived uneasily alongside one another and tension would often lead to outbreaks of violence between different groups, fighting like ferrets in a bag. The empire tried to keep the peace, but it was barely possible in a racially and ethnically diverse society.

One of the major divisions (at least when seen from a Jewish perspective) was between Jews and Gentiles. Jews were used to thinking of Gentiles as unclean, worshippers of the false pagan gods, polytheistic idolaters. They and their ways were to be avoided as much as possible. The Jewish law was an elaborate means of reinforcing separateness. Contact with anything unclean could be washed away through ceremonial washings, in the *mikveh*, or special baths built for the purpose. Food laws ensured that Jews only ate specially prepared food and avoided meat that might have been involved in pagan worship.

The concept of pollution by what is unclean was particularly strong in the Judaism of Paul's time. Jews habitually avoided the gymnasium, the circus and the theatre, in case they were polluted by contact with Gentile ways. Conversely, the Gentile Romans thought of the Jews as eccentric, and a little strange. Sometimes they were viewed with mere amusement or indifference, though tolerated as exempt from the demand to worship the gods at the temples, as they had never done so (unlike Christian converts who were mostly former pagans who had abandoned their religious duties of worshipping the gods).

At other times, relationships were more strained. Tensions between Jews and Gentiles sharpened after 66 AD when a series of incidents in Jerusalem served to rouse Jewish anger, just when the new emperor Vespasian was feeling the need to show some steel by repressing the troublesome and awkward Jews. All this led of course to the destruction of the great Jewish Temple in Jerusalem in AD 70, a disaster from which Judaism in Jerusalem never quite recovered.

The Jewish law was the boundary line that marked off the two communities – Jews were those who kept the law. Gentiles were those who did not. But this was only one of the divides that ran through Roman life. There was the great social divide between the slaves and their owners, fuelled by the perennial fear of the wealthy minority that the slaves would revolt, bringing chaos in its wake.

There were the perennial differences between male and female. There was ethnic friction between Scythians, Parthians, Elamites, Macedonians, Thracians, Romans and the many different types of barbarians. There were social divisions between the high- and low-born, the inevitable jealousies and backbiting between classes in a highly strat-ified, yet socially mobile society.

This is a picture of the human race that is all too familiar. Yes, there are occasional periods of peace and relative harmony, but over its millennia of existence, humanity has been prone to warfare and mutual destruction time and time again. Ancient societies (including ancient Israel of course) reek of blood and battle, many of them seeing war as honourable and noble. Modern conflicts differ only by the sophistication of the weaponry and the numbers of people we are able to kill.

Unifying a divided world

In that context, we find in the book of Ephesians a quite remarkable statement from a first century Jewish writer. Through the death of Christ, God has brought about a new world where Jew and Gentile were reconciled: 'His purpose was ... to reconcile both of them to God through the cross, by which he put to death their hostility'. Referring to the unclean Gentiles, he writes: 'you who once were far away have been brought near by the blood of Christ.' Gentiles, who were alienated from the true Creator God, the God of the Jews, far away from all the privileges of membership of Israel, had now been included at the very heart of God's own people.

When Christ submitted himself to death on the cross, it is as if he, as the representative of the human race, had taken all of that old, weary, conflict-ridden existence, with the inevitability

175

of constant friction and strife, and plunged it into the cold tomb. The old humanity, marked by division and conflict had died. And then the miracle had taken place: a new humanity had arisen.

The resurrected Christ was a new kind of person altogether, one in whom all the old divisions were no longer relevant, where the dividing lines between slave and free, male and female, Jew and Gentile no longer mattered. Instead there was 'one new humanity' (Eph. 2.15), reconciled and restored in relationship to God, the Creator. The Risen Jesus is still human but in a transfigured way, no longer defined by the particularities of his incarnate form: a new kind of human being.

More than this, the Christians in Ephesus to whom this letter was written are said to have been raised together with Christ (Eph. 2.6) – they are now part of this new humanity. They are literally new people, with a new calling over them.

The cross and resurrection therefore open up a new possibility: a new way of being human. A new community is born in which the old divisions are no longer decisive. The entry point is not being born into any ethnic group or possession of social privilege. It is merely baptism, by which the same death and re-birth is symbolized and enacted – the death of the old humanity and the birth of a new one. These baptized people are now reconciled to God and thus called to live out this new kind of human life, working at creating a community in which such ethnic, social and gender differences, while bringing colour and variety, are no longer sources of tension, because the core identity of the community is found in its common life in Christ.

Breaking down walls

Another metaphor comes into view here too: the dividing wall of hostility that separated Jew from Gentile had now been broken down (Eph. 2.14). Defensive and offensive walls were all too common in the ancient world as they are in ours. One in particular that may have been in mind here was the one at the heart of the Temple in Jerusalem that divided the Court of the Gentiles from the Court of the Israelites, with a wall beyond which Gentiles were not allowed to pass. Divisions in the mind and heart are frequently expressed in concrete, whether the barricades that divided Protestant from Catholic in Northern Ireland,

177

the Berlin Wall separating west from east, or the so-called 'Security Wall' that divides many modern-day Israelis from the Palestinians who live in the West Bank. Walls sometimes give security, yet they cut us off from one another, allowing divisions to grow deeper, stereotypes to harden and misunderstanding to grow.

In Christ, says the book of Ephesians, the ultimate dividing wall that separated humanity from God has been dismantled, just as on that remarkable day in 1989 when the Berlin Wall was stormed and torn down by the crowds who gathered to finally do away with that hated symbol of division. In the same way, the spiritual wall that separated different groups within first century society, such as Jew and Gentile, had also been broken down. Rather than two separate kinds of human being – Jew and Gentile – there was now one – a new humanity in Christ.

And this has happened specifically through the cross. The purpose of God was 'to reconcile both of them to God through the cross, by which he put to death their hostility.' The law that divided Jew from Gentile with circumcision as the indelible sign that marked off the Jew from the Gentile, along with the food laws and ritual washings – all these 'commands and regulations' had been set aside after the death of Jesus on the cross. The death of Christ had made this division no longer relevant, because now, membership of the people of God came not through being ethnically Jewish, but by having faith in Christ who died for the sins of the world.

More than this, in the context of the constantly simmering hostility between different ethnicities in Roman cities, Paul's words that in this new self, this new identity, 'there is no Greek or Jew, circumcised or uncircumcised, barbarian, Scythian, slave or free, but Christ is all, and in all' (Col. 3.11) were truly radical.

Division is still with us. We still live with deep divisions between Shi-ites and Sunnis, black and white, Palestinians and Israelis, divorced parents who squabble over children, egos that cannot live together in the workplace. Walls exist everywhere, and the strongest ones are usually made of emotions and ideas, rather than concrete or steel. These are the prejudices that make one person think they are naturally better than another, the assumptions that cause us to keep our distance.

179

Just imagine for a moment the pain caused not only by large- scale conflicts that hit newspaper front pages, but also those small petty enmities that fester in our relationships, the barriers that divide us from one another.

Equality and difference

How does the cross render these divisions irrelevant? Through that ultimate act of self-sacrifice, a new world has come into being, the wound of creation has been healed, the world is reconciled to God and God to the world, the divisions of humanity are overcome. Before the cross, there are no privileges. It makes not the slightest difference whether a person is a wealthy billionaire, a subsistence farmer, a respectable accountant or an elderly pensioner approaching the end of life. All are created, all are guilty, and all are forgiven and accepted in exactly the same way. This is the place at which all divisions fade into the background. Before the cross, everyone is equal. The cross of Jesus is the means by which we are reconciled to God. Christ, the Son brought peace with God, 'access to the Father by one Spirit' (Eph. 2.18) through his death on our behalf.

The idea of equality is of course, a common one in the modern world. It is one we rather take for granted. We live in an egalitarian age, yet one which is so more in theory than in practice. Yet where did this idea of equality come from? Studying ancient cultures reminds us that they were not at all egalitarian: Chinese emperors literally had the power of life and death over their subjects. Roman emperors likewise did exactly as they wished to their subjects. Plato's vision of the ideal society still had barbarian slaves doing the hard manual labour for the Republic, and Aristotle thought some people were simply born to slavery. Despite political advances in ancient Greek thought, the idea of equality certainly did not come from there.

The idea of the equality of all people is deeply embedded in many of us, but it is by no means obvious. In fact, casual observation of most human societies would suggest otherwise: most are very unequal. If we go on the *prima facie* evidence, people are far from equal and some are higher, more privileged and favoured than others. It is in fact a strongly counter-intuitive thing to assert that all people are equal. Such a belief can only come from the sense that they are equal *before something, or someone else.*

Equality is not found within human societies, so it can only come from relation to some external referent that renders all people equal despite apparent differences in ability, fortune or role. Polytheistic religions tend to foster unequal societies, as the many different gods give for many different origins and valuations of people. It is no accident that polytheistic Hinduism, despite its great wisdom and deep spirituality, has fostered a caste system that condemns countless people to poverty and effective slavery.

Equality can only be found with reference to a single origin: people can only be equal when they come from the same source, with the same value, which is why it is the monotheistic religions that have tended to foster the more egalitarian societies.

Jürgen Habermas, the German philosopher, one of the most respected thinkers in the modern world, although not a Christian, writes: 'Egalitarian universalism, from which sprang the ideas of freedom and social solidarity, of an autonomous conduct of life, and emancipation, is the direct heir to the Judaic ethic of justice and the Christian ethic of love ... To this day, there is no alternative to it.'[1]

Where did the idea come from that we are all equal? It grew originally out of the Jewish idea that each human being is the creation of a good and loving God, not an accidental by-product of warfare among the gods, as the ancient Babylonian myths put it, and subsequently, from the Christian idea that we are all equally objects of God's love, shown once and for all through the cross of Jesus, which reconciles us to the one true God before whom we all stand side by side.

The Church as the community of change

At the foot of the cross, the ground is level. No-one is privileged, no-one is better or worse than another. It is the place where differences are overcome, because it is the place where we are oriented back towards our Creator before whom the differences that we take so seriously

---

1 J. Habermas (2006). *Time of Transitions*. Cambridge: Polity. p. 150f.

are rendered irrelevant. Yet of course, the death of Jesus has not instantly brought about a new world, a new humanity, with the ancient divisions overcome. Many modern societies have espoused the ideal of egalitarianism, yet those societies remain as divided and conflict-ridden as ever. The new humanity that the cross and resurrection have brought into being is an invitation rather than a conclusion, a destination, not an arrival.

Not all differences are the same. This doctrine of the new humanity in Christ is neutral on identity, yet discriminating in morality. The new humanity in Christ is a destination as well as a possession. Christians are called to grow into this new humanity in Christ through a disciplined life of growth in virtue, not an absence of it. Differences of ethnicity, race and employment matter not. Differences of moral maturity do. The Church is to be a community in which such moral growth can take place, where this new kind of humanity can take root in us and develop. As a result it is a place where the standards are to be kept high. It is a community in which makes every effort to make it possible to live a life of forgiveness, patience, purity, generosity, forbearance, chastity, self-control and love.[2] This is why the New Testament epistles so often give lists of moral qualities which are to be sought, and those to be avoided.

In Colossians chapter 3, Paul lays this vision out quite clearly. The Church is a community which is ruthless when it comes to the marks of the old humanity: 'Put to death, therefore, whatever belongs to your earthly nature: sexual immorality, impurity, lust, evil desires and greed, which is idolatry ... anger, rage, malice, slander, and filthy language' (vv. 5–8). Why? Because Christians are those who have been clothed with a new humanity, a new self, which is 'being renewed in knowledge in the image of its Creator' (v. 10).

These habits serve to divide people from one another. They breed a competitive, combative spirit, which is a betrayal of the new humanity, in which 'there is no Gentile or Jew, circumcised or uncircumcised, barbarian, Scythian, slave or free, but Christ is all, and is in all' (v. 11). Instead,

2 Of course chastity is not the same as celibacy – a marriage can be sexually active but chaste, in the sense of faithful. Chastity simply means sex in its proper place.

the Church places the highest value on the culti-
vation, not of fame, wealth or physical beauty,
the characteristic concerns of modern affluent
societies, but instead on 'compassion, kindness,
humility, gentleness and patience' (v. 12), precisely
the kind of qualities that build community, rather
than destroy it. They are to learn to 'bear with
each other and forgive one another if any of you
has a grievance against someone. Forgive as the
Lord forgave you. And over all these virtues put
on love, which binds them all together in perfect
unity' (vv. 13–14).

In our meditations on the cross, we have come
back again and again to love. The cross is a
revelation of God because it is the ultimate
demonstration of self-sacrificial love, which is the
heart and nature of God. The community that is
brought into being by the cross that breaks down
the walls that divide people from one another, is
to be a place where those very people can learn
the art of self-sacrificial love, where they can
practise compassion.

This is a vision of a community of moral purpose and
intentional behavioural change. Sadly, it looks very
different from the way a lot of churches conduct

their business. There are not many churches that are marked by a serious commitment to moral and spiritual growth, offering a focused set of practices that enable and foster this kind of personal transformation. Dallas Willard writes of how many churches focus on the Great Commission to 'make disciples of all nations', but are also marked by the 'Great Omission', whereby they have routinely failed to give serious attention to the second half of the verse at the end of Matthew's gospel: 'teaching them to obey everything I have commanded you.'[3]

'More often than not' he writes, 'faith has failed, sadly enough, to transform the human character of the masses, because it is usually unaccompanied by discipleship and by an overall discipline of life such as Christ himself practised. As a result, when faced with the real issues of justice, peace and poverty, what is called faith in Christ has often proved of little help other than the comfort of a personal hope for what lies beyond this life.'[4]

3 D. Willard (1988). *The Spirit of the Disciplines: Understanding How God Changes Lives.* London: Hodder & Stoughton. p. 16.
4 Ibid. p. 230.

Church often feels irrelevant to many contemporary people because it fails to provide real answers to these wider social issues. What is needed is not another set of political or ideological proposals to combat poverty or social exclusion, but specifically a way of life that effectively offers an alternative to a life of conspicuous consumption and social division. The Church is intended to offer not another set of ideas, but another way of living.

According to Paul, the home of this new humanity in Christ is the Church. This community of people, drawn together by faith in Christ was always intended to be a mixed community. At one stage, Paul risks his entire career over this issue. The apostle Peter was happy to allow Jews and Gentiles to eat separately at the common Christian meal, to placate those who wanted to keep the distinction clear between Jew and Gentile within the early Christian communities.[5]

Paul confronted the great Peter, revered in the early Christian world as the confidant of Jesus himself, because as far as Paul was concerned,

5 Gal. 2.11–21.

Peter was implicitly allowing the divisions of a broken world to be reproduced in the Christian Church. This was not a minor issue over which they could agree to disagree: it was a betrayal of the very nature and calling of the Church as the place where the world could find its reconciliation, and where ordinary people could learn to be reconciled to each other.

If the Church is anything, it is intended as a nursery for the new humanity. Nurseries are places to which children are entrusted in order that they can grow in a safe and healthy environment into their full stature. They are not meant to just do child-minding; they are small communities of development and maturing. We use the same word 'nursery' for the place where plants are kept in greenhouses, until they are ready to be re-planted in gardens. The whole idea is that of a space where people (and plants) can grow into their full potential and ripeness.

The Church is a place where we are to learn to overcome the perennial divisions of the old humanity, to learn to love those that are different, and spur each other on to a new life of Christ-like grace, purity and holiness. Churches are to be like nurseries, or schools, which actively care for, nurture and develop people into the new humanity in Christ. John Calvin combines these images of the Church as a nursery and a school, using the familiar Patristic image of the Church as a mother:

> For there is no other way to enter into life unless this mother conceive us in her womb, give us birth, nourish us at her breast … Our weakness does not allow us to be dismissed from her school until we have been pupils all our lives. Furthermore, away from her bosom one cannot hope for any forgiveness of sins or any salvation … it is always disastrous to leave the church.[6]

The Church is both a mother who carefully sees that her children grow up into all they have the potential to be. It is also a school where her children learn the lessons that equip them for life in the world into which they are to be released in due course. The Church is a nurturing and learning community, preparing her members for

6 Calvin, *Institutes* IV.1.4.

life in the new heavens and the new earth, the place where resurrected humanity will be found. A Christian dare never leave the Church because it is the place where Christ is found, where the spiritual nourishment that he gives can be gained, and where the believer can be fed through word, sacrament, fellowship and all the other means of grace, so that they grow into this new kind of human being, marked off not by enmity and partisanship, but harmony and self-sacrificial love.

Of course, the Church, no less than the world, has its fair share of enmity, disagreement and conflict. Reflecting the new humanity in Christ is no automatic thing, but has to be learnt. And it starts by learning who one's own fellow-Christians are. Paul has a phrase for how Christians are to see one another, especially those they disagree with or dislike. The other is a 'brother for whom Christ died' (1 Cor. 8.11). The baptized, believing person next to me in church whose theology I disapprove of, whose political opinions I disagree with, whose cultural habits I don't understand, is my brother or sister, a member of the same family, the object of the same parental love that God has for me, a person for whom Christ died. How can

I then fail to treat them with the reverence and respect that such a standing demands?

The Church therefore exists as a place where reconciled humanity is displayed. This is why the unity of the Church matters so much. A disunited Church cannot bear effective witness to the day when God will bring all things together under Christ, when the work of the cross is seen in its completeness in bringing together a divided humanity.

As the place where God brings a broken world together, the Church is also therefore to be always active in the work of reconciliation in the world.

To take one example, *Musalaha* (which means 'reconciliation' in Arabic) is a Christian movement seeking to bring reconciliation between Israelis and Palestinians, based on the insight that reconciliation comes through the death and resurrection of Christ, in whom all the fundamental divisions of humanity have been overcome.

Among other things, it takes groups of young Israelis and Palestinians into the desert, a place where God met with the Patriarchs and many a prophet in the past, where Jesus' own unique identity as the Son of God was revealed. The desert is a neutral space where new possibilities emerge. By bringing people together, slowly the prejudices and misunderstandings can begin to dissolve.

Shadia Qubti, who works with *Musalaha* says: 'I believe in grassroots movements starting with smaller groups that come from the people. I believe as followers of Christ we have a lot of work to do. If we can establish unity among us, between Israelis and Palestinian Christians first, I think that will have a domino effect within our countries and regions. But first we have to try to get along together as a smaller community, as a prototype that this works. Christ is able to do what the world is not able to do.' *Musalaha* is small, tiny – just 800 people involved in reconciliation projects. It is just one of many such initiatives throughout the world, based on the belief that in Christ reconciliation is possible. Yet as such it is one of these small signs that points to the new humanity in Christ.

The Church knows the secret of the future destiny of humanity – which it is to be re-made in the image of the resurrected Jesus, beyond all the usual divisions and conflict that mark 'normal' life as we know it. Therefore it stands under a calling to work as far as it can for the unity and harmony of the human race. The Church's place in the conflicts of the world is not on the side-lines, scolding or even weeping, but instead at the heart of those conflicts, working to see reconciliation overcome enmity.

That position of mediating and reconciling is very often a painful one, and it brings us back, full circle, to the cross. Christ, as the mediator between God and creation, stretches out his arms to bring them together, yet his outstretched arms are nailed to a cross. This is what mediation and reconciliation costs. Perhaps the Church is never more truly itself than when it is busy reconciling enemies, healing rifts, enabling harmony, taking a cross-shaped posture in the world.

9

THE CROSS AND LIFE

Early on the first day of the week, while
it was still dark, Mary Magdalene went
to the tomb and saw that the stone
had been removed from the entrance.
(Jn 20.1)

For what we preach is not ourselves,
but Jesus Christ as Lord, and ourselves
as your servants for Jesus' sake. For
God, who said, "Let light shine out
of darkness," made his light shine in
our hearts to give us the light of the
knowledge of God's glory displayed in
the face of Christ.

But we have this treasure in jars of clay
to show that this all-surpassing power is
from God and not from us. We are hard
pressed on every side, but not crushed;
perplexed, but not in despair; persecuted,
but not abandoned; struck down, but
not destroyed. We always carry around
in our body the death of Jesus, so that

the life of Jesus may also be revealed in
our body. For we who are alive are always
being given over to death for Jesus' sake,
so that his life may also be revealed in our
mortal body. So then, death is at work in
us, but life is at work in you. It is written:
"I believed; therefore I have spoken."
Since we have that same spirit of faith, we
also believe and therefore speak, because
we know that the one who raised the
Lord Jesus from the dead will also raise
us with Jesus and present us with you
to himself. All this is for your benefit, so
that the grace that is reaching more and
more people may cause thanksgiving to
overflow to the glory of God. Therefore
we do not lose heart. Though outwardly
we are wasting away, yet inwardly we are
being renewed day by day. For our light
and momentary troubles are achieving
for us an eternal glory that far outweighs
them all. So we fix our eyes not on what
is seen, but on what is unseen, since what
is seen is temporary, but what is unseen is
eternal. (2 Cor. 4.5–18)

Life ends in death. That, it seems, is the one certainty about this life. One hundred per cent of people die one day. It will happen to you and it will happen to me. Thankfully we do not know the date of our death. Perhaps if we did, it would be too much to bear. There are a number of websites that promise to calculate the date of your death. Just enter your age, general state of health, gender and so on, and some mysterious calculation will do the rest. Yet part of us is reluctant to know – if we knew a date it would somehow make the whole thing more real and certain. Not knowing means we can put off the thought as long as possible.

Meanwhile we rush around trying to make the most of the time. Why? Because subliminally, we know we don't have forever. We use calendars and clocks to chart the passing of time, because we know it is limited, that it is running out on us, and that today will never return. Our time will come, as we say. As the German theologian Helmut Thielicke put it, 'Behind such very ordinary phrases and facts stands the appalling circumstance that hour by hour we realise that we must die, that we have only a limited time.'[1]

We have built into us an instinct of decline and fall. We chart the rise of empires and we chart their inevitable fall. Decay or entropy is built into the world. We make things, they get broken and we throw them away. We watch food decay if we leave it beyond its sell-by date – decay and death seems the end of the story.

It seems common sense. Yet as we have seen, the cross turns common sense on its head. And no more so than here. Because, faced with the truism that life leads towards death, Christian faith begs to differ. Instead it boldly asserts that death leads towards life.

The reason for this belief is of course that after the cross came the resurrection. The cross was not the last word. In that sense the cross is something of a semi-colon not a full stop, a hiatus not a terminus. Christian faith believes, against all intuition and instinct, that death ends in life.

1 H. Thielicke (1964). *How the World Began: Sermons on the Creation Story.* Cambridge: James Clarke. p. 176.

An eternal weight of glory

Paul was a Pharisee. They were among the strictest of the various Jewish sects in the first century, guarding the ancient traditions of keeping the law. He could presumably have had a fairly successful career as a rabbi within the Pharisaic tradition, or even as something of a scholar, as a Scribe. Yet life had turned out very differently for him since the day he was confronted by the risen Jesus during a routine trip north to Damascus. In this letter to the church in Corinth that so often made him reflect back on the cross of Christ, he thinks of himself, not as a religious dignitary, a respected civic leader of a faith community, but as a cracked and broken 'jar of clay'. He had seen the death of all his plans and intentions, so that from that dramatic day onwards, the main focus of life was not his career, ambitions, identity or reputation, but Jesus Christ.

As he reflected back over his experience of life as a follower of the crucified Christ, often it had felt like death. He had flogged himself around the different cities of Asia Minor, trying to plant small communities of Jesus-followers, teaching them to love one another, break bread and share wine, to baptize and to worship at the start of each week.

He had worked, walked, prayed, written, taught, sweated, worried about these churches. He had been kicked around the Mediterranean basin, been shipwrecked, beaten, imprisoned, or as he puts it here in the letter, 'hard pressed, perplexed, persecuted, abandoned, struck down.'

If there is anything that might make a person doubt their faith, it is sometimes the experience of being a Christian. Teresa of Avila the Spanish mystic was once on a tiring, weary journey to one of the convents in her Order when she was thrown from the cart she was riding in as the horse bolted. She is said to have cried out 'Lord, if this is how you treat your friends, I'm not surprised you don't have many!'

All this is true. The Christian life sometimes feels like slowly dying. And yet that is not the whole story. While Paul recognizes death at work in him, he also recognizes something else going on. He senses another power at work, something hidden, mysterious but nonetheless real. Yes we were afflicted, he says, but we were never quite crushed. We were driven to despair sometimes, but always sensed we were not entirely alone. We were beaten, but never quite destroyed.

The effect was also almost physical: 'outwardly we are wasting away, yet inwardly we are being renewed day by day.' His body was growing weaker with age and exhaustion, not to mention the physical whippings he had taken. Yet inwardly, a new dynamic was at work making him younger not older, renewed not diminished. The death of Jesus was somehow carried around in his body, and yet at the same time the life of Jesus was present too.

This change was happening not just in him, however. It was taking place in the churches that occupied his mind so much as well. 'Death is at work in us but life in you' he writes (v. 12). All those long days walking from place to place, waiting around for ships, the struggles in prayer, the hours spent explaining the basics of the faith in letters or in person, were paying off. They were bearing fruit as more and more people heard the message, came to believe it, and found hope, forgiveness and a new joy.

Paul sees the pattern of death and resurrection being played out in his own life. Yet this experience of Paul's – of sowing in tears and reaping in joy – is just a small echo that points both backwards and forwards. It points back to the cross and resurrection of Jesus. Paul describes his struggles as like carrying around the 'death of Jesus' in his body, so that at the same time, the 'life of Jesus' might be seen in these small successes in his life of planting and growing churches.

Yet it also points forward, to something he sees happening in the entire cosmos itself. Paul writes of an 'eternal glory that far outweighs' his troubles. He fixes his eyes not on what is seen (the process of decay leading inexorably to death) but what is unseen (the coming renewal of all things).

As a result, every answered prayer, every instance of healing, every burst of praise, every act of self-sacrificial love is not a 'raging against the dying of the light', as the poet Dylan Thomas put it, but a sign of new world that is coming. They become the first flowers of spring, the aroma of home on a long journey.

This all seems very hard to believe, set against every funeral ever held, every empire that has fallen. Sam Harris writes: 'Every one hundred million years or so, an asteroid or a comet the size of a mountain smashes into the earth, killing nearly everything that lives. If ever we needed proof of nature's indifference to the welfare of complex organisms such as ourselves, there it is. The history of life on this planet has been one of merciless destruction and blind occasional renewal.' Against such a background, what reason might there be to hope that death leads to life?

Dying to rise

In another place, Paul addresses this very question. Back in Corinth, a church we have visited several times in the past chapters, he faces some members of the congregation who doubt the reality, or have not grasped the significance of resurrection. In chapter 15 of his first letter to the church, he tackles head-on those who say 'there is no resurrection of the dead' (v. 12). These presumably are the same ones who ask the gently mocking question 'what kind of body will resurrected people have?' (v. 35). The assumption behind the question is that when bodies die, they decay and that is the end of it. If you look closely, he argues, you can in fact see another pattern going on in the world than the one of entropy or decay.

Take a look at seeds. When a sower or a gardener plants a seed or bulb in the ground, it looks to all intents and purposes as if it has died. It disappears, and for months on end, nothing is seen of it. In fact, part of it does begin to decay. Yet decay is not the only thing happening. Germination starts. And out of the planted seed comes a green shoot, then a stalk, and then the full ear of corn. Now of course, a field of corn looks nothing like a bucket of seed. A daffodil looks nothing like the bulb that was planted in the ground. It looks as if they are entirely different things. And yet they are related, and continuous with each other. It is not that one vanishes and entirely replaces the other, but that one emerges from the other. It is just like this, Paul suggests with the difference between our current physical bodies and our future resurrection bodies.

In fact it describes well the difference between Jesus' crucified body and the one encountered by the women in the garden on the first Easter day. When Mary saw the risen Jesus, she didn't recognize him, thinking it must be the gardener or someone else (Jn 20.15). On the road to Emmaus, disciples who knew Jesus well also did not recognize him either, and this new body of Jesus appears to be capable of walking through locked doors and thick walls (Jn 20.19). The risen body of Jesus is different from, but continuous with his earthly body, just as a flower is continuous with but different from a seed.

Paul gives another example. Is it hard to imagine different kinds of bodies? Well, consider the differences between the flesh of humans, fish, birds and land animals. Think of the planets. Even bearing in mind his pre-modern understanding of physical matter, we can still conceive of different kinds of mass or energy, such as what physicists call dark matter, antimatter, black holes, electro-magnetic radiation and so on. It is a failure of the imagination to believe there can only be one kind of body: the mortal physical flesh of human beings.

Confirmation of Paul's point comes from a surprising source. Towards the end of *The God Delusion*, Richard Dawkins draws attention to our rather stunted human imagination. He writes 'our brains are not equipped to imagine what it would be like to be a neutrino passing through a wall in the vast interstices of which that wall really consists, nor can our understanding cope with what happens when things move close to the speed of light. ... Evolution in middle worlds ill-equipped us to handle very improbable events but in the vastness of astronomical space or geological time, events that seem impossible in middle world turn out to be inevitable.'[2]

In other words, Dawkins hints that there could be a different order of things from the one we are used to. Might it be, for example, that the resurrected Jesus might be a picture of that future, who came into our world at a specific moment of history to reveal to us the new heaven and the new earth that one day God will bring about?

In both of these examples, Paul hints at another law at work in the physical universe, signs of another trajectory of history, flowing not from life into death, but the other way round. In fact, when you look around, you see this principle everywhere. The whole natural world is built upon it – death and rebirth. Life on the planet could not continue without it. It is not surprising that many of the early religions in the Ancient

2 Dawkins, R. (2007). *The God Delusion*. London: Black Swan.

Near East were fertility religions, displaying this fascination with the process whereby what dies in the autumn and winter comes to life again in the spring and summer.

The problem with the fertility religions is that that they got things the wrong way round. They saw the rhythm of the seasons, and its echo in human sexuality as the origins of new life, as the source of life rather than the means by which it is propagated. Instead, these processes were, all along, only a sign pointing to the true source of life: the God of creation who raised Jesus his Son from the dead, an event which indicates the final and total breaking of the power of that downward pull of decay which always fought against the renewal of life, and tried to undo it. The death of the seed to give birth to the plant was a signpost pointing to something else much larger: the Resurrection of the Son of God who died, in order to give birth to a new humanity, a new world.

Death the path to life

For Paul, as he thinks back on the resurrected Jesus, whom he met on that journey to Damascus in an encounter which had turned the whole trajectory of his life around, we cannot become what we are intended to be unless we die first. Our bodies cannot be transformed into resurrection bodies until they pass through the valley of the shadow of death. Because Jesus has trod this path before him, death no longer holds the terrors of nothingness, the fear of oblivion, which overshadows life with the possibility that it was all pointless, but instead, death becomes the means through which those who are in Christ, identified with him in his death, lose all that holds them back in this life.

The process of dying still holds its fears, but death itself becomes a friend. It becomes the means by which we lose that sense of being stuck in time, with its inevitable cycle of life and death. It ushers us, not into an endless series of rebirths, but into a final death and rebirth into Life itself in which death is no more – it becomes part of the past not the future.

The hymn 'All Creatures of our God and King', a paraphrase of Francis of Assisi's Canticle to the Sun, summons the whole of creation to praise God: Father, Son and Holy Spirit. Wind, Moon, Water, Earth, Humanity are all called to join their voices to the song of praise. Then there comes a quite remarkable verse. It goes like this:

> And thou most kind and gentle Death,
> Waiting to hush our latest breath,
> O praise Him! Alleluia!
> Thou leadest home the child of God,
> And Christ our Lord the way hath trod

Death is summoned to praise God. No longer is it a fearful enemy, to be dreaded and shivered at. Instead it becomes a guide, leading the child of God home to the Father, walking the same path trodden by Jesus himself.

So what needs to happen to us in order for this to be our future? Nothing other than a complete transformation. As Paul puts it:

> Flesh and blood cannot inherit the
> kingdom of God, nor does the perishable
> inherit the imperishable. Listen, I tell
> you a mystery: We will not all sleep,
> but we will all be changed—in a flash,
> in the twinkling of an eye, at the last
> trumpet. For the trumpet will sound,
> the dead will be raised imperishable, and

> we will be changed. For the perishable
> must clothe itself with the imperishable,
> and the mortal with immortality.
> When the perishable has been clothed
> with the imperishable, and the mortal
> with immortality, then the saying
> that is written will come true: "Death
> has been swallowed up in victory."
> (1 Cor. 15.50–4)

We can sense he is struggling for language here, to describe something indescribable. It is, finally, a mystery, yet what is clear is that there must be transformation, not evolution. We can think that somehow we are fine as we are, just needing a little fine tuning here and there. This text suggests something more radical is needed. We need to be *changed*. The seed of who we are now, body and soul, must die, in order that it may be transformed into something else, just as the bulb must die in order for the flower to grow.

And that begins here and now. Back in chapter 4 we thought about how baptism, the beginning stage of the Christian life, indicates a new identity through a death of the old and the rebirth of the new. Becoming and being a Christian is much more like dying and being reborn that it is like a slow gradual improvement through strenuous moral effort. For the new self to be born, the old self has to die, that self-will, the approach to life that places my agenda before anyone else's, the sense that I can do what I want with my life, the illusion that I am in fact the centre of the universe, that I am God.

There can be no negotiation with that old self – it has to go, full stop. It will of course rear its head over and over again, pleading to be allowed back, but must be slapped down where it belongs, until the day when it will finally be gone for good. This principle remains true of everything that we have, everything that we value. If we hold onto it, we will lose it. If we let it go, it can be reborn into something pure and beautiful.

It is the choice that every parent faces. When the child is small, it needs the parent to survive. As the baby grows into a child then a teenager, the parent needs to learn to let go, otherwise he or she will smother their offspring, leaving them incapable of growing into the mature adult they have the potential to be. If the process is negotiated in a healthy way, relationships between parents and grown-up children can be the most satisfying and wonderful things, yet only if this process of letting go take place, only if there is this kind of dying in order for the relationship to be reborn.

Whether it is money that needs to be given away, talents that need to placed at the service of those who need them most, or children that need to be let go, in order to enable them to become what they have the potential to be, there is no way round this rule of life: 'Whoever does not take up their cross and follow me is not worthy of me. Whoever finds their life will lose it, and whoever loses their life for my sake will find it' (Mt. 10.38–9).

This life is not the dress rehearsal for the life to come – it is more significant than that. Yet it is perhaps the first scene of the first act. To think the play is over at that stage to leave the theatre when it is only just begun, is a huge mistake. To think this life is all that there is, is an even bigger one. The cross of Christ, and its counterpart the Resurrection, tell us that the secret of life is found exactly in this pattern of death and resurrection that we see in Jesus, the Son of God.

212

C. S. Lewis writes: 'If we take the imagery of Scripture seriously, if we believe that God will one day give us the Morning Star and cause us to put on the splendour of the sun, then we may surmise that both the ancient myths and the modern poetry, so false as history, may be very near the truth as prophecy. At present we are on the outside of the world, the wrong side of the door. We discern the freshness and purity of morning, but they do not make us fresh and pure. We cannot mingle with the splendours we see. But all the leaves of the New Testament are rustling with the rumour that it will not always be so. Some day, God willing, we shall get in.'[3]

3 C. S. Lewis (2001). *The Weight of Glory and Other Addresses*. London: Harper Collins

BIBLIOGRAPHY

Augustine (1991). *Anti-Pelagian Writings.* Edinburgh: T & T Clark.

Bauckham, R. (1998). *God Crucified: Monotheism and Christology in the New Testament.* Carlisle: Paternoster.

Charry, E. (1997). *By the Renewing of Your Minds: The Pastoral Function of Christian Doctrine.* New York: Oxford University Press.

de Botton, A. (2004). *Status Anxiety.* London: Hamish Hamilton.

de Lubac, H. (1986). *The Splendour of the Church.* San Francisco: Ignatius.

Eusebius (1965). *The History of the Church.* London: Penguin.

Forde, G. O. (1997). *On Being a Theologian of the Cross: Reflections on Luther's Heidelberg Disputation 1518.* Grand Rapids: Eerdmans.

Gorman, M. J. (2001). *Cruciformity: Paul's Narrative Spirituality of the Cross.* Grand Rapids: Eerdmans.

Green, J. B. and Baker, Mark D. (2000). *Recovering the Scandal of the Cross.* Downers Grove: IVP.

Habermas, J. (2006). *Time of Transitions*. Cambridge: Polity.

Hengel, M. (1977). *Crucifixion*. London: SCM Press.

Krakauer, J. (1996). *Into the Wild*. New York: Pan Books.

Kreeft, P. (1992). Back to Virtue. San Francisco: Ignatius Press.

Moltmann, J. (1974). *The Crucified God*. London: SCM.

Murphy-O'Connor, J. (1996). *Paul: A Critical Life*. Oxford: Oxford University Press.

Nietzsche, F. (1996). *On The Genealogy of Morals*. Oxford: Oxford University Press.

Pogoloff, S. M. (1992). *Logos and Sophia: The Rhetorical Situation of 1 Corinthians*. Atlanta: Scholars Press.

Rabinow, P., ed. (1984). *The Foucault Reader: An Introduction to Foucault's Thought*. London: Penguin.

Taylor, C. (1989). *Sources of the Self: The Making of the Modern Identity*. Cambridge: Cambridge University Press.

—(1991). *The Ethics of Authenticity*. Cambridge, MA and London: Harvard University Press.

Tomlin, G. (1999). *The Power of the Cross: Theology and the Death of Christ in Paul, Luther and Pascal.* Carlisle: Paternoster.

Tomlin, G. (2006). *Spiritual Fitness: Christian Character in a Consumer Culture.* London: Continuum.

Tomlin, G. (2007). *The Seven Deadly Sins and how to Overcome Them.* Oxford: Lion Hudson.

Willard, D. (1988). *The Spirit of the Disciplines: Understanding How God Changes Lives.* London: Hodder & Stoughton.